ROCKY MOUNTAIN
NATIONAL PARK

DOREEN GONZALES

MyReportLinks.com Books

an imprint of

Enslow Publishers, Inc.

Box 398, 40 Industrial Road
Berkeley Heights, NJ 07922
USA

MyReportLinks.com Books, an imprint of Enslow Publishers, Inc. MyReportLinks®
is a registered trademark of Enslow Publishers, Inc.

Library of Congress Cataloging-in-Publication Data

Gonzales, Doreen.
  Rocky Mountain National Park : adventure, explore, discover / Doreen Gonzales.
    p. cm. — (America's national parks)
  Summary: "A virtual tour of Rocky Mountain National Park, with chapters devoted to the history
of this region, history of the park, plant and animal life, environmental problems facing the park,
and activities in the area"—Provided by publisher.
  Includes bibliographical references and index.
  ISBN-13: 978-1-59845-096-5 (hardcover)
  ISBN-10: 1-59845-096-4 (hardcover)
  1. Rocky Mountain National Park (Colo.)—Juvenile literature. I. Title.
  F782.R59G66 2009
  978.8'69—dc22
                                    2007039043

Printed in the United States of America

10 9 8 7 6 5 4 3 2 1

To Our Readers:
Through the purchase of this book, you and your library gain access to the Report Links that specifically back
up this book.
The Publisher will provide access to the Report Links that back up this book and will keep these Report Links
up to date on **www.myreportlinks.com** for five years from the book's first publication date.
We have done our best to make sure all Internet addresses in this book were active and appropriate when
we went to press. However, the author and the Publisher have no control over, and assume no liability for,
the material available on those Internet sites or on other Web sites they may link to.
The usage of the MyReportLinks.com Books Web site is subject to the terms and conditions stated on the
Usage Policy Statement on **www.myreportlinks.com**.
A password may be required to access the Report Links that back up this book. The password is found on
the bottom of page 4 of this book.
Any comments or suggestions can be sent by e-mail to comments@myreportlinks.com or to the address
on the back cover.

♻ Enslow Publishers, Inc., is committed to printing our books on recycled paper. The paper in every book
contains 10% to 30% post-consumer waste (PCW). The cover board on the outside of each book contains
100% PCW. Our goal is to do our part to help young people and the environment too!

CONTENTS

MyReportLinks.com Books
Great Books, Great Links, Great for Research!

The Internet sites featured in this book can save you hours of research time. These Internet sites—we call them *"Report Links"*—are constantly changing, but we keep them up to date on our Web site.

When you see this "Approved Web Site" logo, you will know that we are directing you to a great Internet site that will help you with your research.

Give it a try! Type http://www.myreportlinks.com into your browser, click on the series title and enter the password, then click on the book title, and scroll down to the Report Links listed for this book.

The Report Links will bring you to great source documents, photographs, and illustrations. MyReportLinks.com Books save you time, feature Report Links that are kept up to date, and make report writing easier than ever! A complete listing of the Report Links can be found on pages 118–119 at the back of the book.

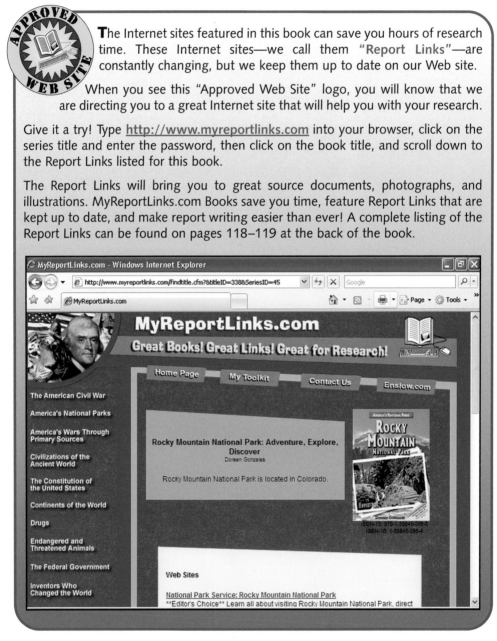

Please see "To Our Readers" on the copyright page for important information about this book, the MyReportLinks.com Web site, and the Report Links that back up this book.

Please enter RMP1640 if asked for a password.

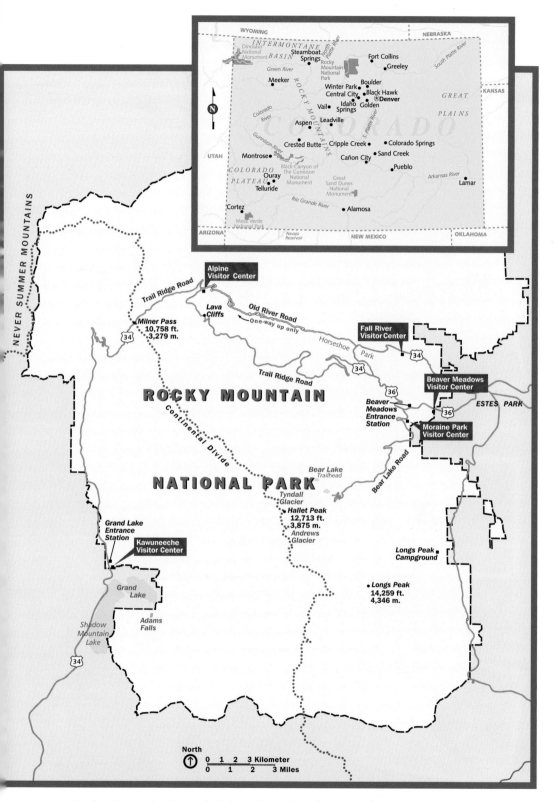

Rocky Mountain National Park is located in the central part of northern Colorado. The large map is a visitor's map from the National Park Service. The inset shows where RMNP is in relation on the rest of Colorado.

- Rocky Mountain National Park was established on January 26, 1915.

- The park is located in north central Colorado, 80 miles (129 kilometers) northeast of Denver, Colorado.

- Rocky Mountain National Park encompasses 416 square miles (1,077 square kilometers).

- Trail Ridge Road, the highest paved continuous highway in the United States, runs through the park. So does the Continental Divide, dividing the park into east and west sections.

- Rocky Mountain National Park contains 88,000 acres (35,614 hectares) of some of the most pristine alpine tundra in the world.

- The park includes 114 mountains higher than 10,000 feet (3,048 meters). Its highest mountain is Longs Peak at 14,259 feet (4,346 meters). Its lowest point is 7,840 feet (2,390 meters) above sea level.

- Annual precipitation on the east side of the park is 13 inches (33 centimeters). The west side receives an average of 20 inches (51 centimeters).

- Some of the most commonly seen animals in Rocky Mountain National Park are chipmunks, ground squirrels, mule deer, elk, bighorn sheep, black-billed magpies, and chickadees.

- The park provides a home to the greenback cutthroat trout and the Canadian lynx, two animals on the federal threatened or endangered species list. The bald eagle, a bird that recently came off the threatened or endangered list, also lives there.

- Favorite activities in Rocky Mountain National Park include hiking, wildlife viewing, climbing, camping, horseback riding, picnicking, fishing, cross-country skiing, and snowshoeing.

- East-side visitor centers include the Alpine, Beaver Meadows, and Fall River Visitor Centers and the Moraine Park Museum. On the west side there is one visitor center, the Kawuneeche Visitor Center.

- Visitors should be aware of the park's wild, mountainous environment and take precautions to avoid altitude sickness, lightning, falls, hypothermia, avalanches, and dangerous wildlife encounters.

- The park is open year-round, although Trail Ridge Road and Old Fall River Road are closed from fall to spring. Two park entrance stations are located near Estes Park, Colorado. They are the Beaver Meadows and Fall River Entrance Stations. One, Grand Lake Entrance Station is near Grand Lake, Colorado.

- Rocky Mountain National Park attracts nearly 3 million visitors each year.

- As of 2008, seven-day admission was twenty dollars per vehicle.

Chapter

1

Most visitors to Rocky Mountain National Park find the majestic views breathtaking. This is Longs Peak.

The View From the Top

Have you ever been to the top of the world? I am standing there right now. The wind is whipping through my hair and my fingers went numb ten minutes ago. But I can't climb down from my rock perch. The view has hypnotized me.

Below me, forest-covered land rolls in green waves to taller mountains behind it. They are treeless but carpeted in miniature plants. Here and there, red rocks jut from the green and stone towers reach to the sun. Above the softness is rock spotted with pools of snow.

There's snow near me, too. Crusty patches dot the ground and small plants grow around them. Their tiny purple and yellow blossoms seem unaware of the cold. But I shiver and shake. It seems unbelievable that only hours ago I was hot—and thousands of feet lower.

We ate lunch at the bottom of the park near a narrow river. Nearby trees made speckled patches of shade. Bold chipmunks and magpies lurked near our picnic table, just waiting for one of us to drop a crumb. We shooed them away, hoping they would find their own food. A funny black squirrel with pointed ears watched us from a branch.

After eating, my brother and I waded into the water. It was so cold that it stung my feet. Then we climbed into the car to start the long drive up the mountains. The road twisted and turned between pine forests.

Almost halfway to the top, we pulled off the road to look out. Beyond the forests lay a bright green meadow. A brown river cut through it, wandering back and forth as it meandered across the land. Suddenly, I heard a sound in the trees below me. I jumped and shrieked! Was it a bear? Nothing was there except my brother laughing at me.

Back in the car, we started a steady climb up a rocky slope and my ears started popping from the change in altitude. Suddenly the car in front of us stopped. A curly-horned bighorn sheep was standing next to the road. More sheep munched on grass in the valley below. We waved good-bye, but none of them noticed.

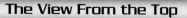

Rocky Mountain National Park was created by volcanoes, with metamorphic rock forming the highest peaks. This Web site presents a 517-photo **Rocky Mountain National Park Virtual Tour**.

EDITOR'S CHOICE

Finally, we made it to the top. I opened the car door and cold air smacked me in the face. I laughed and ran to the stone patio next to the parking lot. I looked over its short stone wall. A pair of eyes were staring back at me; it was a marmot.

My brother pointed into the distance. Several elk were grazing there. When I turned back, my brother was running toward some steps that led even higher. I followed, thinking there must be a thousand. Once I thought we were at the top, but the trail only dipped to rise again. I reached the summit completely out of breath.

A vast space opened before me. Mountains beyond surrounded the horizon. Behind them was another row of peaks, and still another behind those.

A sign said we were 12,005 feet (3,659 meters) above sea level. Actually, I didn't care about the number. I was at the top of Rocky Mountain National Park. I was on top of the world!

THE PARK IN THE MOUNTAINS

The Rocky Mountains are the longest mountain chain in North America. They stretch 3,000 miles (4,827 kilometers) from Alaska to the southern United States. Yet the Rockies are not an unbroken chain. They are long groups of mountains separated by plateaus, lowlands, passes, and rivers. Each group is called a range.

The Front Range of the Rocky Mountains runs through central Colorado. Rocky Mountain National Park (RMNP) is a 416-square-mile (1,077-square-kilometer) chunk of its northern stretches.

It has the highest average elevation of any national park in the lower forty-eight states. One-third of the park lies above 11,500 feet (3,505 meters), or what is known as the timberline, or tree line.[1] Several park mountains rise over

13,000 feet (3,962 meters). The highest, Longs Peak, reaches 14,259 feet (4,346 meters).

The Continental Divide enters Rocky Mountain National Park at its northwest corner and travels toward the center of the park. From there it moves south. This divide is a ridge of mountains that serves as a division of watershed drainage. It indicates the direction that water flows. Waters on the east side of the divide flow to the Atlantic Ocean, while waters on the west side run to the Pacific.

The divide acts as another kind of partition in the park. Its peaks create a wall that blocks precipitation moving from the west to the east. This makes the west side of the park wetter than the east side. Because of this, differences in vegetation and wildlife exist on each side of the divide. The Continental Divide, therefore, forms a natural borderline between the east and west sides of the park.

TUNDRA

Not surprisingly, the highest altitude continuously paved highway in North America runs through Rocky Mountain National Park.[2] Trail Ridge Road travels from one side of the park to the other. On the way, it climbs to more than 12,000 feet (3,658 meters) and crosses alpine tundra.

Tundra is a Russian word meaning "land without trees." The park's tundra starts at 11,400 feet

About.com
International
Biosphere
Reserves

Rocky Mountain National Park has been designated an International Biosphere Reserve. Find out background on the nomination process and links to entries on the twenty-nine parks so designated.

Access this Web site from http://www.myreportlinks.com

(3,475 meters). Specifically, it is alpine tundra because it is caused by elevation. Although this land is too cold for trees, plants abound. Most are shorter than 6 inches (15 centimeters).

Some of the same plants that grow on the park's tundra are found on the arctic tundra. Other plants are unique to the park. The tundra covers more than 100 square miles (259 square kilometers) of the park's land.

DIVERSITY

Of course, not all of Rocky Mountain National Park is as high as the tundra. Its lowest land lies about 7,700 feet (2,347 meters) above sea level.

This means within the park elevations vary by more than 6,000 feet (1,829 meters).

This elevation difference supports a large variety of life. Most plants that live at 8,000 feet (2,438 meters) cannot survive in higher altitudes. Other plants thrive there. The same is true of animals. The park, therefore, is filled with a large assortment of plants and animals.

Due to this diversity, Rocky Mountain National Park has been designated as an International Biosphere Reserve. Biosphere reserves are places that scientists have deemed important because of their exceptional examples of the world's ecosystems. There are less than four hundred International Biosphere Reserves in the world.

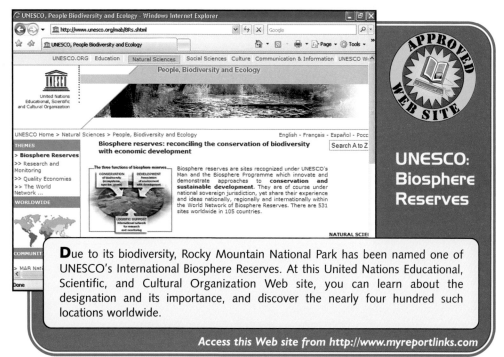

UNESCO: Biosphere Reserves

Due to its biodiversity, Rocky Mountain National Park has been named one of UNESCO's International Biosphere Reserves. At this United Nations Educational, Scientific, and Cultural Organization Web site, you can learn about the designation and its importance, and discover the nearly four hundred such locations worldwide.

Access this Web site from http://www.myreportlinks.com

The ecosystems in Rocky Mountain National Park are representative of the Southern Rocky Mountains, most notably the alpine tundra. They are managed to preserve their integrity, particularly as development intrudes upon their borders.

CLIMATE AND WEATHER

Rocky Mountain National Park has more than three hundred days of sunshine each year. Even so, it is a land of temperature extremes. At lower elevations, summer temperatures average in the 70°F (20°C) range. As elevation increases, temperatures fall and the wind picks up. In general, temperatures drop about three degrees for every

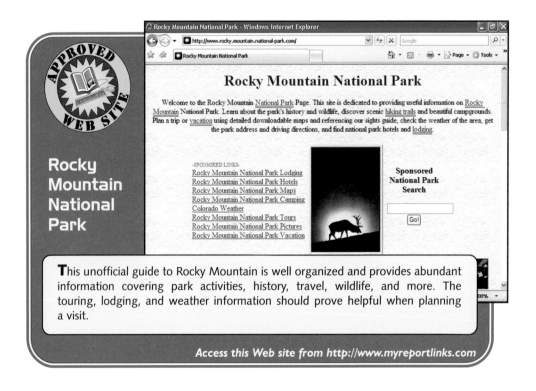

Rocky Mountain National Park

Rocky Mountain National Park

Welcome to the Rocky Mountain National Park Page. This site is dedicated to providing useful information on Rocky Mountain National Park. Learn about the park's history and wildlife, discover scenic hiking trails and beautiful campgrounds. Plan a trip or vacation using detailed downloadable maps and referencing our sights guide, check the weather of the area, get the park address and driving directions, and find national park hotels and lodging.

-SPONSORED LINKS-
Rocky Mountain National Park Lodging
Rocky Mountain National Park Hotels
Rocky Mountain National Park Maps
Rocky Mountain National Park Camping
Colorado Weather
Rocky Mountain National Park Tours
Rocky Mountain National Park Pictures
Rocky Mountain National Park Vacation

Sponsored
National Park
Search

Go!

This unofficial guide to Rocky Mountain is well organized and provides abundant information covering park activities, history, travel, wildlife, and more. The touring, lodging, and weather information should prove helpful when planning a visit.

Access this Web site from http://www.myreportlinks.com

1,000 feet (305 meters) of elevation gain.[3] But differences can be more dramatic.

Winter days are cold and windy. At the lowest elevations temperatures average in the 30°F (−1°C) range. Temperatures are much colder at the mountaintops, though. Here the thermometer often dips below 0°F (−18°C). Furthermore, day and night temperatures can vary greatly. Warm 70°F (21°C) days frequently become 40°F (4°C) nights.

The east side of Rocky Mountain National Park is semiarid. It averages about 13 inches (33 centimeters) of precipitation each year. The west side receives about 20 inches (51 centimeters). Elevation helps determine whether precipitation falls as rain or snow. In the winter, the high country is covered in snow. Yet snow can come anytime at the mountaintops. Snow in the lower elevations begins in October and lasts until May.

The nights are clear. Away from city lights, the sky is black and dotted with a seemingly impossible number of stars.

MOUNTAIN VISITORS

Nearly 3 million people visit Rocky Mountain National Park each year.[4] They come from every state as well as many foreign countries. Most visitors leave having had an unforgettable experience in one of America's most scenic places.

Chapter

2

A geological phenomenon called uplift caused the creation of the Rocky Mountains and the beautiful landscape of Rocky Mountain National Park.

Before There Was a Park

Two billion years ago, Rocky Mountain National Park was covered by a sea. Centuries passed, and the weight of the water pressed the sand on the sea's bottom into stone. Rock created this way is called sedimentary rock.

At times, volcanoes near the ancient sea threw lava into the water. It hardened and became sandwiched between layers of sedimentary rock. Sometimes the rocks were pulled under the earth's crust. Heat and pressure inside the earth changed them into metamorphic rocks. Some of these were pushed back onto the earth's surface.

Two kinds of metamorphic rock from this period can be found in the park today. One is a marbled black, white, and gray rock called *gneiss*. Another is a darker rock called *schist*.

For millions of years, the sedimentary and metamorphic rocks lay on the sea's bottom. At times, magma from inside the earth bubbled into the water. It hardened into pink granite. This granite is found in several places on the east side of the park.

THE MAKING OF MOUNTAINS

About 300 million years ago, the earth's crust began moving. Huge pieces of land collided into others. Land buckled and folded. Sometimes land was thrust skyward. This is called uplift. Uplift built mountains in the region.

More centuries passed, and the mountains were eroded into hills. Then the entire process began again. Once more, land was lifted into mountains that were eroded. Seas came and went, depending on the shape of the land.

About 145 million years ago, brontosaurus, stegosaurus, and other reptiles roamed parts of Colorado. By 100 million years ago, Rocky Mountain National Park was a shallow sea with mountainous islands. Shell fossils from this era have been found on the west side of the park. Dinosaurs probably wandered the sea's shoreline.[1]

The last period of uplift began about 70 million years ago. During this time, huge blocks of metamorphic rock were thrust upward. Slabs of gneiss and schist from the seafloor slid over newer rock. They were pushed to the very top of the land. These slabs form the highest peaks in the park.

Then about 25 million years ago, volcanoes added more mountains to the region. Eruptions threw out lava and rock, building the Never Summer Mountains. They run along the western edge of the park. Hardened lava from these eruptions can still be seen at Lava Cliffs and Milner Pass.

→ GLACIAL CARVING

Glaciers reshaped the area 2 million years ago. At this time, the earth's climate cooled. Great sheets of ice called glaciers covered the land. A period like this is known as an ice age.

Much of Rocky Mountain National Park was glaciated during this ice age. Gravity pulled on the ice fields, drawing them downward. As the ice

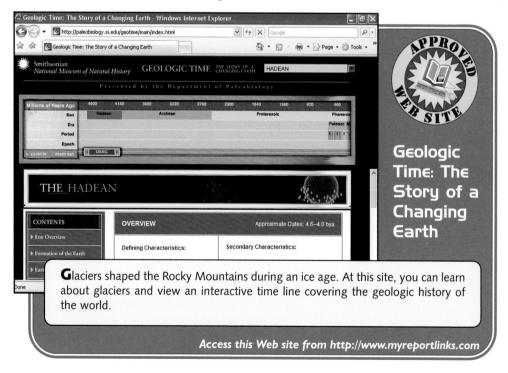

Geologic Time: The Story of a Changing Earth

Glaciers shaped the Rocky Mountains during an ice age. At this site, you can learn about glaciers and view an interactive time line covering the geologic history of the world.

Access this Web site from http://www.myreportlinks.com

moved, it cut into mountainsides and carried away huge chunks of rock. This created deep canyons and U-shaped valleys such as Moraine Park, Horseshoe Park, and Glacier Gorge.

After thousands of years, the earth warmed and the glaciers melted. Rocks inside the ice were released into new homes. Rock-filled fields created by melting glaciers are called moraines. There are several moraines in the park. Moraine Park, for instance, is full of boulders left by an ancient glacier.

More ice ages followed. During the most recent, a glacier 500-feet (152 meters) thick covered Horseshoe Park. Ice caught under the rocks here formed Sheep Lakes.

This ice age ended about twelve thousand years ago. Yet there are still more than one hundred glaciers in the park.[2] Most are small. Two, Andrews Glacier and Tyndall Glacier, are popular hiking destinations.

⊖ THE FIRST HUMANS

The first humans entered the area now known as Rocky Mountain National Park as the glacial period of the last ice age ended. These ancient people probably crossed the Bering Land Bridge and came south along the east slope of the Rocky Mountains, following game. They hunted bison, mammoth, and other animals. Stone arrows that

In the 1700s, Arapaho Indians moved into the land where Rocky Mountain National Park is now located. Many places in the park have Arapaho names.

tipped their spears have been found in the park. Portions of today's Trail Ridge Road were known to be a frequented route for nine thousand years.

By six thousand years ago, ancestors of the Ute Indians were living on the west side of the park. Sometimes they climbed high to hunt. Their stone arrowheads, knives, and spear points have been found along the Continental Divide.

AMERICAN INDIAN LIFE

Remnants of native game drives have also been found on park peaks. These low stone walls were built in the shape of a funnel. Men herded game into the large end. Then it is likely that women and children hiding behind the walls shouted at the animals. This kept the game moving toward the narrow end of the drive where hunters were waiting to kill them.

Sometimes the prehistoric people traveled from one side of the mountains to the other. Two of today's park roads, Trail Ridge Road and Old Fall River Road, follow the routes they used.

During the next thousands of years, other American Indian tribes wandered into the area. But until the end of the eighteenth century, the Ute were the most populous.

Then, during the late 1700s, large groups of Arapaho moved into the region. They had been forced from their Minnesota homes by the United

States' movement west. The Ute and the Arapaho often fought. Even so, the Arapaho stayed. Today, many park locations have Arapaho names.

⇒ FUR TRAPPERS AND TRADERS

European Americans first appeared in the area during the early 1800s. Most came to trap beaver and other animals. Their furs and pelts were sold to businesses in the East. Many trappers made friends with the American Indians in the area.

In 1820, Army Major Stephen H. Long led an expedition to the foothills east of the Rocky Mountains. On his journey, he saw a peak so high that at first he thought it was a cloud. The mountain was unique in height and shape and Long used it as a landmark. This mountain became known as Longs Peak.

When gold was discovered in Colorado in 1858, prospectors flocked to the region. Some found gold, but many did not.

One unsuccessful miner gave up prospecting to ranch instead. In 1860, Joel Estes and his family built a log home in an empty valley on the east side of what is now Rocky Mountain National Park. A large, open area in the mountains is often called a park, so this valley became known as Estes's Park. In time, the name was shortened to Estes Park. Soon other ranchers were trickling into the area. People were settling on the west side of the mountains, too.

In 1865, Abner Sprague and his mother, Mary, became the first white settlers on land that would one day be Rocky Mountain National Park. They built a ranch in what is now called Moraine Park.

Most area ranchers were able to raise enough cattle to earn a living. Yet life in the high mountain valleys was harsh. Some settlers did not stay long. The Estes family, in fact, left the region in 1866. Their name stayed, however.

JOHN WESLEY POWELL

In 1868, John Wesley Powell led an exploration of the area. Powell was a Civil War veteran who had lost an arm in battle. When he left the army, he became a professor at an Illinois college. Intrigued by the unexplored West, Powell organized an expedition to explore the Rocky Mountains and collect specimens for his college. Powell's group became the first documented people to reach the summit of Longs Peak.[3] Soon the mountain was attracting other adventurers.

Sightseers were trickling into the region, too. Englishwoman Isabella Bird visited in 1873. She described the splendor of the Rockies in letters she wrote to her sister. In one, Bird said, "The scenery up here is glorious, combining sublimity with beauty. . . ."[4] Her descriptions were published in a

book called *A Lady's Life in the Rocky Mountains.*
Bird's writings and the accounts of other tourists
advertised the area's beauty to people all over the
world.

THE BIRTH OF TOURISM

Before long, ranchers had tourists knocking at
their doors looking for food and shelter. "The hotel
business was forced on us," Abner Sprague once
called. "We came here for small ranch operations,
but guests and visitors became so numerous, at
first wanting eggs, milk, and other provisions,

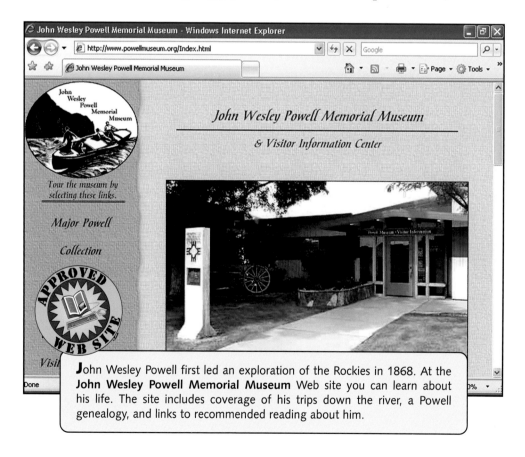

John Wesley Powell first led an exploration of the Rockies in 1868. At the **John Wesley Powell Memorial Museum** Web site you can learn about his life. The site includes coverage of his trips down the river, a Powell genealogy, and links to recommended reading about him.

then wanting lodging, and finally demanding full accommodations, that we had to go into the hotel business or go bankrupt from keeping free company!"[5]

The Spragues weren't the only ones. Since the Spragues' arrival, others had settled in what is now Rocky Mountain National Park. Almost all of the homesteaders ranched, but most depended on additional income from tourists. Each passing year brought more hikers, climbers, and sightseers.

For a short time, the west side of the park had another industry. During the late 1800s, miners came looking for gold. In 1879, Joe Shipler found silver.

LuLu City

By 1882, a town had grown up around Shipler's mine. It was called Lulu City. The town had five hundred residents, several stores, and a regular stagecoach run. Yet little good ore was found there, so people began to leave. The town was empty by 1884. Today only traces of a few log cabins remain.

The mountains also attracted big-game hunters. They killed so many elk, gray wolves, and grizzly bears that these animals would soon be extirpated (locally extinct).[6] The fish population was also dwindling.

28

The human population, on the other hand, was increasing. A village had grown up in Estes Park. It had a community building, a post office, and even a few hotels. In 1909, wealthy businessman Freelan O. Stanley, famous for his steam-powered automobiles, opened a luxurious hotel there. The Stanley Hotel was built on a hill that overlooked the little town. It had a banquet hall and a billiard room. Sun parlors looked out to the mountains.

A town was also developing on the west side of the mountains. More and more visitors were building homes along the shores of Grand Lake. The area was rapidly becoming a summer resort surrounded by ranches.

Businesses inside the park also catered to tourists. Moraine Park was filled with cabins and lodges. There was even a swimming pool and golf course there. Fall River Lodge hosted tourists in Horseshoe Park. Phantom Valley Ranch lodged visitors on the west side. Hotel owners built roads to their lodges and trails to scenic mountain spots.

Back then, the land was part of the Medicine Bow Forest Preserve. As such, ranchers could graze cattle on the land. People could also log the timber.

An Idea is Born

Yet the unchecked use of natural resources and the loss of wildlife concerned many citizens. Many loved the wild land. They also depended on it for their livelihood. This made them determined to protect it. One day, a forest official made a suggestion. He told some residents that they should make the area into a wildlife refuge.[7] Many people liked the idea.

Some took it even further. They wanted the region made into a national park. The country already had several national parks, including Yellowstone and Mount Rainer. These were places so special that the nation's leaders wanted everyone to be able to enjoy them. They also wanted to protect their natural features for future generations.

A national park seemed like the perfect idea. A park would give local residents economic security by attracting tourists from around the world. Furthermore, it would be maintained and operated

▽ In the early 1900s, resort towns were popping up in the area surrounding the park. One of them was Estes Park. This panoramic photo was taken in 1919.

PANORAMA VIEW OF ESTES PARK VILLAGE, COLORADO

No. 304 C

by the federal government. Perhaps best of all, park status would protect the beauty and natural resources that made their home so special. A committee was formed to promote the idea.

ENOS MILLS

The most enthusiastic member of the Park committee was Enos Mills. Mills had come to Estes Park when he was fourteen years old. By the time he was sixteen, he had built a cabin that looked out to Longs Peak.

Mills embraced his mountain home with all of his heart and soul. He led walks, gave nature talks, and guided people to the top of Longs Peak. He also traveled whenever he could. On one of his trips, Mills met the famous naturalist, John Muir. Muir introduced Mills to the formal concept of conservation.

▲ *Isabella L. Bird included this illustration of her home in the Rocky Mountains in her memoir* A Lady's Life in the Rocky Mountains, *published in 1882.*

Mills believed deeply in protecting natural resources. He felt that people needed places where they could experience nature. He once said, "Within national parks is room—glorious room—room in which to find ourselves, in which to think and hope, to dream and plan, to rest and resolve."[8]

From 1910 to 1915, Mills crossed the nation seeking support for a national park in his corner of the Rockies. Mills spoke to every group that would listen. He even talked to people in the U.S. Congress.

⊜ AREA IMPROVEMENTS

While Mills lobbied for a park, others worked to improve the region. One group wanted to bring elk back into the area. They got the chance in 1913 when a Wyoming herd was thinned. Twenty-nine of the elk were sent by train to Lyons, Colorado. Special trucks took them to Estes Park. At first they were put in a pen near the Stanley Hotel. Then the elk were herded into Horseshoe

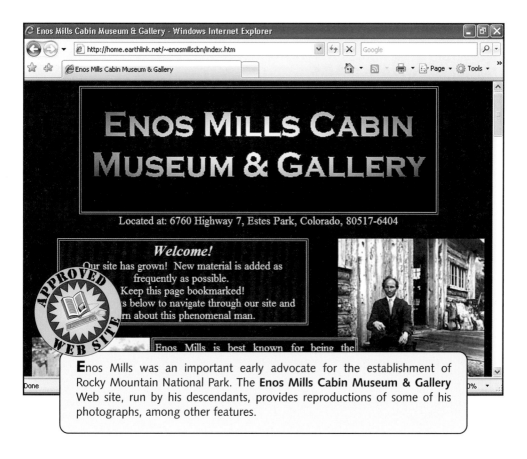

Enos Mills was an important early advocate for the establishment of Rocky Mountain National Park. The **Enos Mills Cabin Museum & Gallery** Web site, run by his descendants, provides reproductions of some of his photographs, among other features.

Park. This mission was so successful that more elk were brought there in 1915.

In the meantime, the state was building a road across the mountains. It would link Estes Park to Grand Lake. The road would start in Horseshoe Park. It would follow Fall River up the mountain to nearly twelve thousand feet above sea level. From there it would travel down the other side of the mountains to Grand Lake.

Work on what is now Old Fall River Road started in August 1913. Labor was done by convicts from a Colorado prison. They stayed in log cabins in an area now known as Endovalley.

A NEW PARK

As the road was being built, the years of campaigning for a national park began paying off. In 1915, Congress passed the Rocky Mountain National Park Act. This bill made almost 360 square miles (932 square kilometers) of land west of Estes Park the country's newest national park. Rocky Mountain National Park officially came into existence when President Woodrow Wilson signed the bill on January 26, 1915.

Two thousand people attended the park's dedication ceremony that September. Hundreds walked from Estes Park to the celebration in Horseshoe Park. Others came by horseback, wagon, and car.

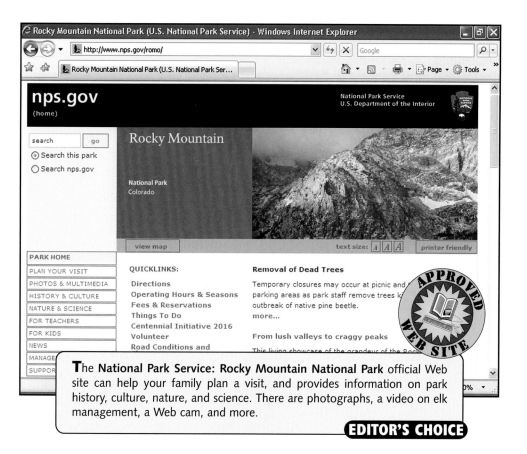

The **National Park Service: Rocky Mountain National Park** official Web site can help your family plan a visit, and provides information on park history, culture, nature, and science. There are photographs, a video on elk management, a Web cam, and more.

EDITOR'S CHOICE

Ladies from the Estes Park Woman's Club hosted the affair. They handed out souvenir buttons and ice cream. Children from the town's school sang "America." Telegrams were read and speeches were made.

One speaker was Enos Mills. He told the crowd, "We should enlarge this park."[9] People have not forgotten Mills's role in creating the new park. Today he is known as the Father of Rocky Mountain National Park.

Chapter

3

Author Doreen Gonzales skies the trails of Rocky Mountain National Park. From the time it was first opened to the public, RMNP was viewed as a great place for winter sports.

The New Park

Soon after Rocky Mountain National Park was established, the federal government created the National Park Service (NPS). This agency would oversee the nation's national parks, including its newest member in Colorado. (Today, the agency protects nearly four hundred areas of natural, cultural, and recreational significance.)

→ THE FIRST YEARS

The NPS's first order of business was improving Rocky Mountain National Park's trails and roads. In addition, there were plans to develop the park for winter sports. Areas for skiing, snowshoeing, ice skating, and tobogganing were planned.

But the park's early budgets were tiny. Its first one barely covered the salary of the park's superintendent and three rangers. Each ranger was paid nine hundred dollars for the year. From this, he had to feed and maintain his own horse.

Even so, improvements were made. The park's first campground opened in 1917. Glacier Basin contained one hundred campsites and was an instant success.

In addition, work continued on Old Fall River Road. It opened in 1920. Its climb up Fall River Pass included a series of switchback turns. Views alternated between looks straight down mountain cliffs to mile-long vistas across Horseshoe Park. Cars soon filled the road.

A NEW ROAD

Unfortunately, Old Fall River Road had problems almost from the day it opened. It was too narrow and steep for many vehicles. Its retaining walls

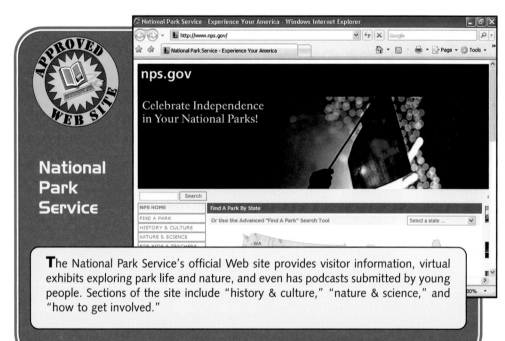

The National Park Service's official Web site provides visitor information, virtual exhibits exploring park life and nature, and even has podcasts submitted by young people. Sections of the site include "history & culture," "nature & science," and "how to get involved."

Access this Web site from http://www.myreportlinks.com

often collapsed and mud slides were frequent. In addition, snow closed the road every autumn. Each spring, it took crews a month to shovel through 25-foot (8-meter) snowdrifts.

So park officials began planning a new road. This one would follow the "Ute Trail," the route the Ute Indians used to travel from the east to the west side of the mountains. Construction on Trail Ridge Road began in 1929.

A BIGGER PARK

In 1930, the U.S. Congress added 22 square miles (57 square kilometers) of land to the park. Now it would include the Never Summer Range. This put the headwaters of the Colorado River and the old mining town of Lulu City inside Rocky Mountain National Park.

In addition, the National Park Service had been buying the privately owned land and lodges inside the park. Many were in Beaver Meadows, Horseshoe Park, and Moraine Park. The buildings on these properties were torn down so the land could return to its natural state.

In 1931, the park's first museum opened. Exhibits inside showed the park's geology and plant and animal life. By the end of 1932 Rocky Mountain National Park had two more museums. One was at Bear Lake and the other at the top of Fall River Pass.

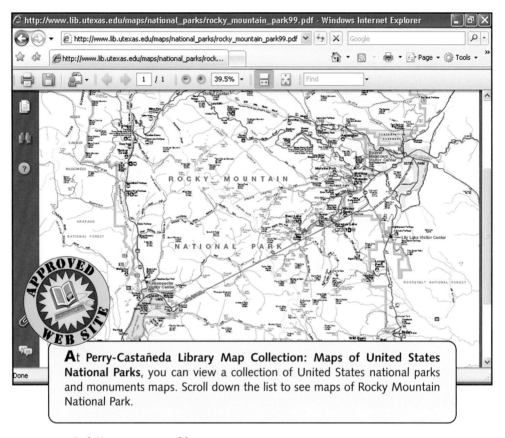

At Perry-Castañeda Library Map Collection: Maps of United States National Parks, you can view a collection of United States national parks and monuments maps. Scroll down the list to see maps of Rocky Mountain National Park.

WILDLIFE MANAGEMENT

During the park's early years, officials made an effort to protect animals from predators. They were especially protective of the elk that had been brought from Wyoming.

So for many years, officials worked to get rid of the mountain lions and bobcats that killed elk and bighorn sheep. At one time or another, these animals were shot, trapped, and even poisoned.[1]

In 1931, a new policy took effect. Now predators were to be treated as a natural and vital part of the park's wilderness. They were not to be harmed unless they were threatening people. This brought an end to all efforts to control predators.

⇒ NEW ROADS

Trail Ridge Road opened in 1932. It was 50 miles (80 kilometers) long and climbed to 12,000 feet (3,658 meters). That summer, four hundred cars used the road each day. On weekends and holidays the count often rose to a thousand per day.[2]

In addition, there was another new road. It stretched from Fall River Entrance to Horseshoe Park, cutting between Sheep Lakes and Bighorn Mountain. This caused a problem for the park's bighorn sheep. They regularly descended Bighorn Mountain to drink from mineral-rich ponds, known as Sheep Lakes. Now they had to cross the busy road to do this. The sheep adapted. Even today visitors can watch as bighorn hop down the mountain slope and wait to skittishly cross the often-busy street.

⇒ CIVILIAN CONSERVATION CORPS

Many other improvements were made in the 1930s. Most were done by the Civilian Conservation Corps (CCC). The CCC was a government program that provided jobs for men who were out of work because of the Great Depression, a very difficult economic slump that began in 1929 and lasted until 1939.

CCC workers built outdoor amphitheaters in Aspenglen, Glacier Basin, and Moraine Park campgrounds. They planted trees and put out fires. They built new trails and improved old ones. CCC workers remodeled a building to make another museum. They also constructed ski and sled runs at Hidden Valley.

The serene setting of Bear Lake. In 1932 a museum opened alongside Bear Lake to help visitors learn more about the park.

The CCC left the park in 1942. But in just under a decade, the workers had completed an immense amount of work. Some experts feel more progress was made in Rocky Mountain National Park during these years than in any period before or since.[3]

THE BIG THOMPSON PROJECT

The late 1930s brought another project to Rocky Mountain National Park. East of the Rocky Mountains lay the Great Plains. It was filled with farms, ranches, and several growing towns. All of these people needed water. Yet water there was scarce.

In 1937, the U.S. Congress approved the Big Thompson Project. It was one of the largest

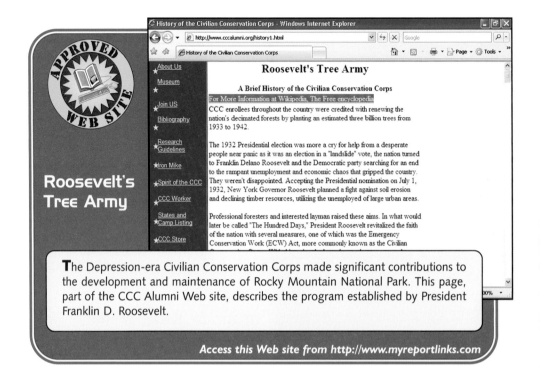

History of the Civilian Conservation Corps - Windows Internet Explorer

http://www.cccalumni.org/history1.html

History of the Civilian Conservation Corps

About Us
Museum
Join US
Bibliography
Research Guidelines
Iron Mike
Spirit of the CCC
CCC Worker
States and Camp Listing
CCC Store

Roosevelt's Tree Army

A Brief History of the Civilian Conservation Corps

For More Information at Wikipedia, The Free encyclopedia

CCC enrollees throughout the country were credited with renewing the nation's decimated forests by planting an estimated three billion trees from 1933 to 1942.

The 1932 Presidential election was more a cry for help from a desperate people near panic as it was an election in a "landslide" vote, the nation turned to Franklin Delano Roosevelt and the Democratic party searching for an end to the rampant unemployment and economic chaos that gripped the country. They weren't disappointed. Accepting the Presidential nomination on July 1, 1932, New York Governor Roosevelt planned a fight against soil erosion and declining timber resources, utilizing the unemployed of large urban areas.

Professional foresters and interested layman raised these aims. In what would later be called "The Hundred Days," President Roosevelt revitalized the faith of the nation with several measures, one of which was the Emergency Conservation Work (ECW) Act, more commonly known as the Civilian

Roosevelt's Tree Army

The Depression-era Civilian Conservation Corps made significant contributions to the development and maintenance of Rocky Mountain National Park. This page, part of the CCC Alumni Web site, describes the program established by President Franklin D. Roosevelt.

Access this Web site from http://www.myreportlinks.com

irrigation projects ever. A huge pipe would be built through the mountains. It would take plentiful water from the west side of the Continental Divide to the drier east side. The irrigation pipe would be almost 10 feet (3 meters) in diameter and 13 miles (21 kilometers) long. At its deepest, it would be 3,800 feet (1,158 meters) below the earth.

The project started on the west side in 1939 with a blast from 144 sticks of dynamite. Soon workers on both sides of the Divide were digging through the mountains. When east-side workers met west-side workers in 1944, the tunnel was less than 1 inch (2.5 centimeters) off.

The first water was sent through the Alva B. Adams tunnel at 11:00 A.M. on June 23, 1947. Three hours later, it emerged on the east side.[4] A crowd of one thousand people had gathered there to see it. Once on the east side, the water was directed through a series of ditches, dams, and reservoirs. These provided water to cities and farms on the Front Range.

Today the tunnel delivers more than 3 million tons of water to the east side each year. Yet the Big Thompson Project does more than irrigate. It also manufactures power. The system has six power plants along its waterways. They produce almost seven hundred million kilowatt hours of electricity a year. This is enough to provide power for one year to sixty thousand families.

MISSION 66

By the 1950s, more and more people were visiting the national parks. But the parks were in poor shape. Most had not been maintained due to the lack of money during the World War II years.

So in 1955, Congress funded a plan to improve the national parks. Part of the plan called for information centers in every park. These new buildings would be called visitor centers. All of the improvements were to be completed by 1966, in time for the fiftieth anniversary of the creation of the

A view from the side of Trail Ridge Road, one of the main roads through the park.

National Park Service. Hence, the plan was called Mission 66.

Rocky Mountain National Park used Mission 66 money to build three visitor centers. One was on the east side at Beaver Meadows. This building's design was based on the work of famed architect Frank Lloyd Wright. Wright believed buildings should blend in with their natural surroundings. The Beaver Meadows Visitor Center would be a one-story building made from area stone.

Another visitor center was built at the top of Trail Ridge Road. Alpine Visitor Center sat at an altitude of nearly twelve thousand feet (3,658 meters). This building was made of stone and log beams. It included a glassed-in viewing area that looked out to the mountains. The third center, Kawuneeche Visitor Center, was built on the park's west side near Grand Lake.

THE 1970S

The 1970s brought a new environmental awareness to the country. Air and water pollution became topics of national concern; so did the preservation of natural resources.

The programs and policies of Rocky Mountain National Park echoed these concerns. Park rules became more protective of the wilderness. Officials worked hard to educate the public about conservation. Park signs, pamphlets, and

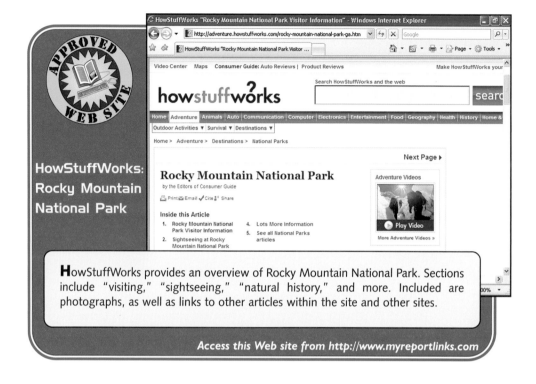

HowStuffWorks:
Rocky Mountain
National Park

HowStuffWorks provides an overview of Rocky Mountain National Park. Sections include "visiting," "sightseeing," "natural history," and more. Included are photographs, as well as links to other articles within the site and other sites.

Access this Web site from http://www.myreportlinks.com

programs stressed the need for people to respect the natural environment.

LAWN LAKE FLOOD

In 1982 natural forces once again changed an area of the park. That July, the dam at the 11,000-foot (3,353-meter)-high Lawn Lake broke. Thousands of gallons of water rushed into the Roaring River and poured down the mountainside. It took 400-ton (363-metric-ton) boulders and 30-foot (9-meter) trees with it.

The water did not stop at the bottom of the hill. The flood hit the Cascade Dam, which also failed, adding more water to the torrent. It tore across the land and washed through Aspenglen campground. Three campers were killed. The water raced on into Estes Park, destroying several businesses and homes.

By the time the flooding stopped, the water had reshaped the area. A scoured rock face now stood where a tree-lined mountain slope had been. At the bottom of the mountain was a deposit of huge boulders and logs. The debris created an alluvial fan, or fan-shaped deposit. The alluvial fan from the Lawn Lake flood is 42 feet (13 meters) thick.

➡ Today's Park

Currently, 95 percent of the park is managed as wilderness, although only 5 percent—the Indian Peaks Wilderness—is officially designated as wilderness. In May 2007 a Colorado congressman proposed a new law that seeks to designate most of Rocky Mountain National Park's backcountry as official wilderness. Such a designation would ensure that the park remains natural and wild for future generations. As of May 9, 2008, the U.S. Senate Energy and Natural Resources Committee unanimously passed legislation that would give most of RMNP wilderness status.

Of course, erosion will keep reshaping the park. The nearly constant wind in the high country eats away at jagged summits. Water seeps into

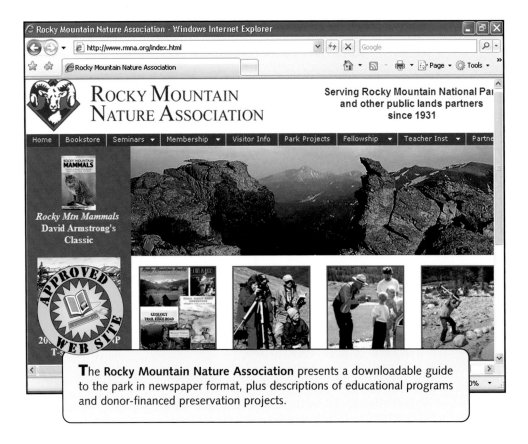

The **Rocky Mountain Nature Association** presents a downloadable guide to the park in newspaper format, plus descriptions of educational programs and donor-financed preservation projects.

rock crevices. When temperatures drop, the water freezes and expands. This sometimes cracks the rock. Cracked rocks fall from slopes, changing the face of the mountain.

Streams cut deeper into the earth. Water flowing down mountains moves boulders and deposits sediments to new places. The park may look very different in centuries to come.

As for today, Rocky Mountain National Park is a wild place of forests and meadows and high mountain peaks. It provides sanctuary to all kinds of plants and animals, including a few threatened or endangered species. Among them are the boreal toad and the greenback cutthroat trout. The bald eagle and the Canadian lynx also find protection here.

The park is a kind of sanctuary for people, too. It is a place of more than 100 pristine lakes, 350 miles (563.3 kilometers) of hiking trails, waterfalls, abundant wildlife, and murmuring streams. Rocky Mountain National Park provides respite for the city-weary and anyone else craving the peace of the natural world.

⊖ A VISIT TO THE PARK

Many tourists begin their visit to Rocky Mountain National Park on the east side from Estes Park. Beaver Meadows Visitor Center is along Colorado Highway 36. Inside the center are a small bookstore and a 3-D model of the park. Rangers provide visitors with information about the weather, wildlife, and area activities.

A short way from the park entrance is the turn to Bear Lake. A little over a mile down Bear Lake Road is Moraine Park Museum. This stone building overlooks the meadow where a golf course once stood. The museum's interactive displays explain the geologic history of the park.

A walk up Bear Lake Road will lead to Sprague Lake, where Abner Sprague once owned a resort. Higher up, Bear Lake offers a number of hiking

options. One trail circles the lake. Popular hikes from Bear Lake include Nymph, Emerald, Dream, Lake Haiyaha, and Flattop Mountain. Popular hikes from Glacier Gorge Trailhead include Mills Lake, Loch Vale, Sky Pond, and Alberta Falls, a waterfall named for Sprague's wife.

Sprague Lake was once home to a resort owned by Abner Sprague, a park pioneer.

Backtracking down Bear Lake Road is Highway 36. The highway climbs upward to Deer Mountain, becoming Trail Ridge Road. Due to snow, Trail Ridge Road is only open from mid-May through mid-October.

Lower Trail Ridge Road winds through pine forests. At Beaver Ponds, a boardwalk leads to beaver-created wetlands. Farther up the road is Hidden Valley. This was once a ski area; now it's a center of activity for sledding. A warming house and picnic area sit at the bottom of the sled runs. A few miles farther up is Many Parks Curve. Beaver Meadows, Moraine Park, Longs Peak, Horseshoe Park, and Estes Park are all visible from this overlook.

Trail Ridge Road then climbs above the trees. A path at Forest Canyon Overlook stretches into the tundra. The road makes a few more twists and turns before arriving at Lava Cliffs. These rocks were deposited millions of years ago during volcanic explosions. The high point of the road is 12,183 feet (3,713 meters), right near Lava Cliffs.

Finally, Trail Ridge Road arrives at the Alpine Visitor Center at 11,796 feet (3,595 meters). A large parking lot flanks the Alpine Visitor Center and Museum. Next door to the visitor center is a gift shop and snack stand.

FALL RIVER ENTRANCE

Visitors can also enter the east side of the park through the Fall River Entrance on Colorado Highway 34. The Fall River Visitor Center opened in 2000 and is just east of the Fall River entrance, outside the park boundary. This center features a discovery room where young visitors can dress up like the early hunters and settlers of the region. It also offers interactive displays and a small bookstore. A large gift shop next door provides souvenir shopping opportunities.

A short way from this entrance is Aspenglen Campground. A bit farther down Old Fall River Road is Horseshoe Park. This valley is named for the boulders a glacier left in a horseshoe shape around the valley's edge. Spring and summer find

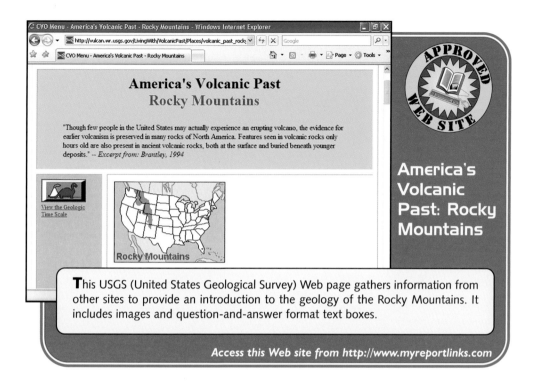

America's Volcanic Past: Rocky Mountains

This USGS (United States Geological Survey) Web page gathers information from other sites to provide an introduction to the geology of the Rocky Mountains. It includes images and question-and-answer format text boxes.

Access this Web site from http://www.myreportlinks.com

bighorn sheep working their way down Bighorn Mountain to drink from Sheep Lakes. Horseshoe Park is also a popular place for elk to gather in the autumn.

At the upper end of Horseshoe Park is the alluvial fan created by the 1982 Lawn Lake Flood. Today the Roaring River tumbles tamely over the mountain on its way to Fall River. A gently sloping path weaves through the flood-deposited boulders and beside miniature beaches.

Continuing up the road is Endovalley, where convicts once bunked while building Fall River Road, now Old Fall River Road. Only a few stones

▲ *The cascading waters of the alluvial fan, which flows into Fall River.*

from their cabins remain. Now a tree-filled picnic area lines the banks of the bubbling Fall River.

Endovalley also marks the entrance to Old Fall River Road. It is only open from July 4 to early autumn and leads in only one direction—up. It is narrow and rough. Yet the Old Fall River Road offers some of the park's most spectacular views.

After many hairpin turns, the road climbs upward to the windswept tundra and ends at the

Alpine Visitor Center. During the summer, elk and marmots are frequent sights. A quarter-mile trail from the parking lot leads to a 12,000-foot (3,658-meter) overlook, offering sweeping vistas of the Mummy Range.

➧THE WEST SIDE

From the Alpine Center, Trail Ridge Road continues westward and downward. A sharp curve leads to a dramatic view of the Kawuneeche Valley. In the summer its bright green is a vivid contrast to the muted colors of the east side. Kawuneeche

National Geographic Travel Guide: Rocky Mountain National Park - Windows Internet Explorer

http://www.nationalgeographic.com/destinations/Rocky_Mountain_National_P

National Geographic Travel Guide: Rocky Mountain Na...

Page ▾ Tools ▾

Main Menu > Rocky Mountain National Park   Scroll Down for Things to See and Do ↴

Rocky Mountain National Park

- Map: Political/Street

Planning Your Trip

- Orientation
- When to Go
- Statistics
- Getting There
- How to Visit
- Activities
- Park Information
- Lodging
- Related Links

Rocky Mountain National Park

Set atop the Continental Divide, Rocky Mountain National Park draws nearly as many visitors as the much larger Yellowstone. It includes the headwaters of the Colorado River and dozens of peaks above 12,000 feet (3,658 meters). Lower-elevation meadows and evergreen forests give way above 11,000 feet (3,353 meters) to a brutal Arcticlike climate where trees cannot

National Geographic: **Rocky Mountain National Park** is a useful page containing background on the park, how to plan a visit, and things to do there. The page also has links to nearby forests, monuments, and wildlife refuges.

means coyote in Arapaho, and on many nights the valley coyotes sing.

Just down the road is the Continental Divide at Milner Pass. To the east, a stream trickles out of Poudre Lake to become the Cache La Poudre River. The Poudre moves eastward into rivers that flow to the Mississippi River. The Mississippi eventually empties into the Atlantic Ocean at the Gulf of Mexico.

Less than a half mile west at Lake Irene are the beginnings of Phantom Creek. This stream flows to the Colorado River. The Colorado then

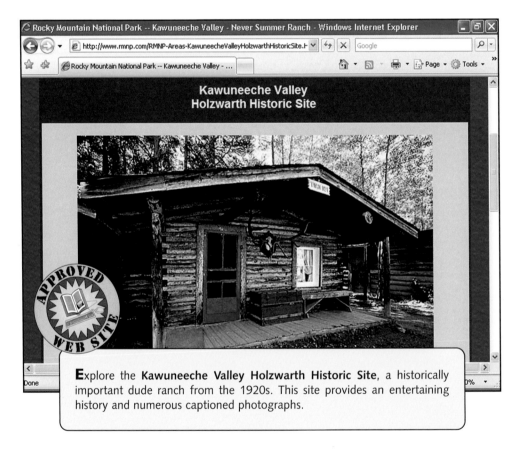

Explore the **Kawuneeche Valley Holzwarth Historic Site**, a historically important dude ranch from the 1920s. This site provides an entertaining history and numerous captioned photographs.

crosses the Southwest by way of the Grand Canyon. It empties into the Pacific Ocean at the Baja Peninsula.

Farther down Trail Ridge Road is Timber Creek Campground. Moose wander through these camp-sites along the Colorado River. A trail from the campground leads to the site of the old Lulu City mine.

Holzwarth Historic Site is the next stop. A dude ranch operated here from the 1920s to the 1970s. Its buildings have been restored to look as they did in the 1920s, when the site—then called Trout Lodge—was visited by anglers. Guests back then paid two dollars a day to stay in a primitive log cabin. "Mama" Holzwarth prepared their hearty meals.

At the bottom of Trail Ridge Road is the Kawuneeche Visitor Center. This small building sits tucked into the trees. It features a bookstore, information desk, and displays of park plants and animals. Several trails begin here.

The highlights of Rocky Mountain National Park can be seen in a few days. It might take a life-time, though, to completely explore the park.

Chapter

4

This mule deer buck is an example of just one of the various species of animals found in the park. Mule deer live in the meadows of the montane zone.

Life in the Park

Rocky Mountain National Park's elevation ranges from 7,700 feet (2,347 meters) to more than 14,000 feet (4,267 meters). This means that three different life zones may be found within the park: the montane zone at 7,500–9,500 feet (2,286–2,896 meters); subalpine at 9,000–11,500 feet (2,743–3,505 meters); and alpine zone at 11,500 feet (3,505 meters) and beyond. A life zone is a distinct community of plants and animals found at a certain elevation. Each elevation supports a unique group of plants and animals.

Of course, life zones are not absolute. Sun exposure, dips in elevation, and vegetation patterns all create microclimates within each life zone. These make unique niches within the larger ecosystem. Of course, no walls or fences separate the zones, and some plants and animals live in more than one.

However, there is much uniformity within life zones. This makes them a useful way to categorize the plants and animals of the park.

⊜THE MONTANE

The lowest and warmest life zone in the park is the montane zone. Summer temperatures average in 70°F (21°C) and can reach into the 80°F (27°C) range. Nights are cooler, and temperatures may drop below freezing. Daytime winter temperatures sometimes dip into the single digits, but the 30°F (−1°C) range is more common.

Ponderosa pine trees thrive in this environment. Ponderosas have a reddish bark that resembles puzzle pieces. Their 5-inch (13-centimeter) olive needles grow in twos and threes.

Ponderosas live for hundreds of years. Some reach 150 feet (46 meters). They grow in small groups with wide spaces between them. Grasses, shrubs, and wildflowers grow under and around them. This understory provides food and habitat for many small animals.

One animal, the Abert's squirrel, lives only in ponderosa forests. It eats the tree's twigs, inner bark, and the seeds inside its pinecones. This squirrel is gray or black with tufted ears.

Bark beetles are common in ponderosas, too. These .5-inch (1.3-centimeter) insects crawl under tree bark and tunnel through the wood. Along with the spruce budworm, mountain pine beetles will eventually destroy the trees.

Lodgepole pine trees also grow throughout the montane zone. These trees grow to 80 feet (24

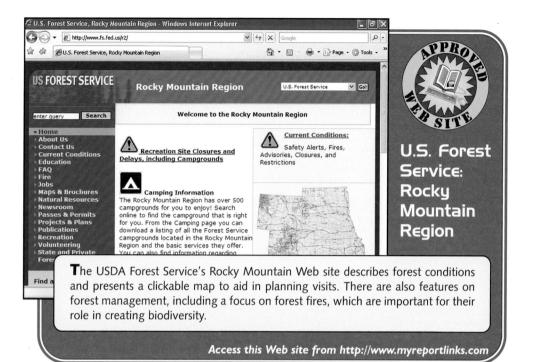

The USDA Forest Service's Rocky Mountain Web site describes forest conditions and presents a clickable map to aid in planning visits. There are also features on forest management, including a focus on forest fires, which are important for their role in creating biodiversity.

Access this Web site from http://www.myreportlinks.com

meters). Yet they are rarely more than 15 inches (38 centimeters) in diameter. The trunks of these tall, straight trees were often used by American Indians to support their tepees. This is how they got the name "lodgepole" pines.

Lodgepoles are especially adapted to survive fire. Their cones are sealed shut by a resin, protecting the seeds inside. Heat from a fire melts the resin and releases the seeds. Lodgepole seedlings sprout quickly in dry, ashy soil.

ASPEN GROVES

Quaking aspens are also common in the montane meadows. Aspens have white bark and roundish green leaves that quiver in a breeze. Their leaves turn bright yellow in the fall.

Aspens spread by sending new trunks up from their roots. New trees can appear 130 feet (40 meters) from a mother tree. All of the tree trunks that come from one tree are considered one organism.[1] This means an entire group of aspen trees can actually be one plant.

Individual aspens live up to 150 years. Aspen roots, though, can live for thousands of years. Aspens also survive forest fires because their roots do not get burned.

The understory of an aspen grove is filled with grasses and wildflowers. These provide food and habitat for small animals like Colorado chipmunks and golden-mantled ground squirrels.

These two animals look alike and are often mistaken for each other. But the golden-mantled ground squirrel is larger than a chipmunk. It can grow to nearly 12 inches (30 centimeters). Chipmunks only grow

 Often mistaken for a chipmunk, golden mantled squirrels are abundant in RMNP.

to 9 inches (23 centimeters). Chipmunks can also be identified by the stripe that goes all of the way across their faces. A golden-mantled squirrel's stripes stop just past its shoulder.

Aspen groves bustle with birds. Woodpeckers drill holes in the soft aspen bark looking for insects. Mountain bluebirds and wrens move into the cavities the woodpeckers leave. The bright red and yellow western tanager also likes aspen forests.

Broad-tailed hummingbirds are another bird of the montane. They are less than 4 inches (10 centimeters) long. They have a bright green back and crown. The males have a bright red collar. Hummingbirds are migrators who arrive in the park in April. By autumn, these tiny birds have moved south.

MONTANE MEADOWS

Meadows dot the montane zone. The meadows on the east side are dry, gentle slopes covered with grasses and shrubs. Wax currant, sagebrush, and kinnikinnick abound. The meadows are also full of wildflowers. Wild raspberry, geraniums, golden banner, and yarrow are common.

Meadows on the park's west side are filled with many of the same species. Yet because they are wetter, the vegetation there is lusher. A few plants are unique to wetter meadows. Pink elephant heads is one such plant. The stem of this flower is filled with bright pink blossoms that resemble two elephant ears and a trunk.

→ MEADOW ANIMALS

Montane meadows attract animals, too. Mule deer feed on its grasses and small plants. This deer's name comes from its large, mule-like ears. Mule deer are about 4 feet (1 meter) tall.

The 10-inch (25-centimeter)-long northern pocket gopher is also common in montane meadows. It carries grass and plants in fur-lined cheek pouches that open on the outside.

Pocket gophers live in burrows. Above the ground, they stay close to their burrow entrance. Underground, though, they dig long tunnels across the meadows. The montane is covered with mounds of soil that gophers have pushed out while making tunnels.

Birds thrive in montane meadows, too. The black-billed magpie is common here. This member of the crow family grows to 20 inches (50 centimeters) in length. It has a black head, breast, and lower belly. Its shoulders and wing feathers are white. The magpie has dark blue inner wings with a long green and blue tail. Black-billed magpies eat insects, seeds, fruit, and nuts. They even stand on the backs of elk, sheep, and deer to eat the ticks off of them.

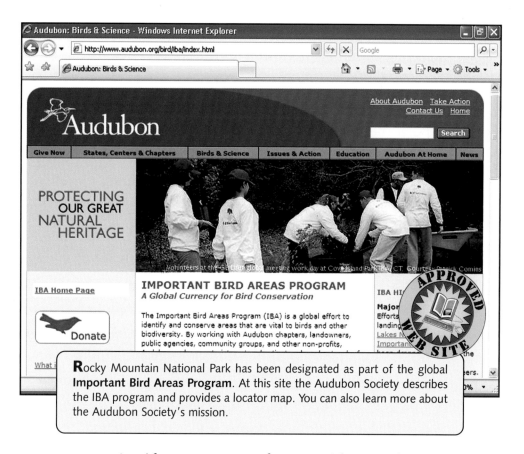

Rocky Mountain National Park has been designated as part of the global **Important Bird Areas Program**. At this site the Audubon Society describes the IBA program and provides a locator map. You can also learn more about the Audubon Society's mission.

A wide assortment of ants, spiders, and mites also thrive in the montane zone. The common blue butterfly and painted lady butterfly are both found here. All of the insects are an important food for many animals. They, in turn, feed on dead animals and plants.

➡ FOXES, BADGERS, COYOTES, AND BOBCATS

The small animals of the montane zone attract larger predators. The red fox is common. This doglike mammal grows to 3 feet (91 centimeters) in length. It has rust-colored fur with a long, bushy white-tipped tail. An expert hunter, the fox likes ground-nesting birds and small rodents.

Badgers live here, too. These grayish brown animals have short muscular legs and long claws. Both help them dig. Badgers are such good diggers they can disappear into the ground in seconds. They eat squirrel, mice, and gophers.

Bobcats also roam Rocky Mountain National Park's montane meadows looking for small rodents. Bobcats' coats are brown with black spots, and they have black bars on their forelegs and tail. Their pointed ears have short tufts of black hair at the tip. They grow to 3 feet (91 centimeters) in length and can weigh up to 30 pounds (14 kilograms).

Coyotes are one of the most adaptable animals in the park. The coyotes found here are a grayish tan. They are about 2 feet (61 centimeters) tall and weigh up to 30 pounds (14 kilograms). Coyotes eat fruit and small animals.

⊜ Top Gun

The park's top predator is the mountain lion. This cat is also called the panther, puma, and cougar. Mountain lions are tan with light patches of fur on their underbodies. An adult can weigh 200 pounds (91 kilograms). Lions can run 70 miles (113 kilometers) an hour and jump 20 feet (six meters).

▲ *The mountain lion is the most dangerous predator in RMNP, yet it is extremely rare for a human to encounter one.*

Mountain lions are rarely seen. Each lives alone, and an adult needs 100 square miles (259 square kilometers) of territory to be comfortable. Mountain lions eat deer, elk, and small animals. They ambush their prey and kill it with a powerful bite at the base of the skull. They then drag the carcass off to bury it in secret. Mountain lions can drag animals seven times their own weight.

Follow these safety rules if you are ever in the area where mountain lions roam: One should never hike alone. Remember to make noise while hiking in mountain lion country. Carry a large stick to make yourself look bigger and more threatening in case you meet a mountain lion on the trail. Do not run away!

THE SUBALPINE ZONE

The subalpine zone lies at 9,000–11,500 feet (2,743–3,505 meters). This higher elevation means colder temperatures and stronger winds. Subalpine summers are short and cool. Winters are long and cold. The subalpine zone receives more than 30 inches (76 centimeters) of precipitation each year. Much of this falls as snow.

Dense forests cover the subalpine zone. Engelmann spruce and subalpine fir are the most common trees. The Engelmann is shaped like a cone. It can grow to 100 feet (30 meters) with a diameter of 30 inches (76 centimeters). It has reddish bark. Colorado blue spruce is the shape of the classic Christmas tree.

The subalpine fir tree grows to 115 feet (35 meters) tall. It has a long, narrow crown of short, stiff branches. Its needles are blue green and turn upward. Its bark is smooth and gray. Juniper shrubs cover the forest understory. Yellow-flowered cinquefoil shrubs grow well here, too.

Wildflowers also thrive in the subalpine. The Colorado columbine favors moist, rocky soil. This

Rocky Mountain National Park | Oh, Ranger! - Windows Internet Explorer

http://www.ohranger.com/rocky-mountain

Rocky Mountain National Park | Oh, Ranger!

Oh, Ranger!

For Answers To All Your Questions™

site search | Go

In Depth

- Rocky Mountain National Park
- 10 Essentials
- Activities & Programs
- At Your Fingertips
- Bighorn Sheep
- Camping at Rocky Mountain
- Continental Divide Trail
- Estes Park
- Flora & Fauna
- Grand Lake
- Hiking Chart
- Histo...

Rocky Mountain National Park

Rocky Mountain National Park

This "park in the sky," which captures the full grandeur of the Rocky Mounta... country's most frequently visited national parks, attracting more than thr... each year. 76 of the great mountains in the park reach elevations of 12... Forests of spruce and fir tower over wide valleys where aspen and wild... streams and lakes. At the highest elevations, above the tree line, is the... alpine tundra, fraught with blizzards in winter and filled with flowered me... this is just 65 miles northwest of Denver! Rocky Mountain National Park o... enormous variety of things to do throughout the year, ranging from all sno...

The **Oh Ranger! Rocky Mountain National Park** site from the American Park Network presents visitor information covering activities, programs, hiking, camping, and more. A photo gallery shows different areas of the park.

delicate-looking lavender and white bloom is Colorado's state flower. Scarlet-colored Indian paintbrush, lupine, and Jacob's ladder are also widespread.

Snowshoe hares find shelter in these forests, too. This medium-sized rabbit is especially adapted to high altitude winters. Its grayish brown summer fur is replaced with white fur in the winter to blend into its environment. Its large hind feet spread out to act like tiny snowshoes for travel atop the snow. Fur on the hare's soles protects it from the cold.

▲ *The three lavender flowers are the Colorado columbine, the state flower. A scarlet-colored Indian paintbrush is behind them.*

Pine martens also live in the subalpine zone. These small members of the weasel family are about 2 feet (61 centimeters) long and weigh up to 2 pounds (1 kilogram). Martens roam the conifer treetops at nighttime hunting squirrels and birds.

Porcupines live here, too. These dark brown rodents can be 3 feet (91 centimeters) long. They eat shrubs, leaves, and grasses. In the winter, they scrape the trees to get at their inner bark. Guard hairs on the porcupine's back and tail have sharp barbed quills that come off easily. This protects them from enemies.

BIRDS OF THE SUBALPINE

Many birds also make their homes in the sub-alpine area. The mountain chickadee is one of the most common birds in the park. This 5-inch (13-centimeter) bird is black and gray with a white eye stripe. Chickadees hide seeds and insects under bark, in pine needle clumps, and in the ground for eating later.

The Stellar's jay also frequents the subalpine. It is the only crested jay in the Rocky Mountains. Its color is a deep iridescent blue. The hermit thrush and pine grosbeak also live among the trees of the subalpine.

BEARS IN ROCKY MOUNTAIN NATIONAL PARK

Black bears dwell among the lower forests of the subalpine. But Rocky Mountain National Park's black bears are not always black. Some are cinnamon in color, some are brown, and some are a light gold. They are about 6 feet (2 meters) long and can weigh up to 400 pounds (181 kilograms).

Black bears eat a variety of food. Their diet includes grasses, fruit, carrion, insects, small rodents, and nuts. In the winter, they go into a deep sleep called torpor, and they stay in dens that they've built under logs or in caves or culverts.

KRUMMHOLZ

A unique forest called krummholz is found high in the subalpine. Krummholz is a German word meaning "crooked wood." Trees in the krummholz are twisted and gnarled. Their trunks and branches have been shaped by the constantly blowing wind. In some areas, the wind creates flag or banner trees. These are trees with branches on only one side of their trunks.

Limber pines grow 30 feet (9 meters) tall. They are often rounded or flat at the top. The name limber comes from the fact that these trees have flexible branches. This bending keeps the branches from breaking in strong winds.

The Clark's nutcracker is vital to limber pines. This black, white, and gray bird measures 11 inches (28 centimeters). When limber pine cones ripen in the fall, nutcrackers pry them open to get the seeds. The birds then bury the seeds for winter feeding.

Nutcrackers forget about many of the seeds they bury. Yet these are not lost. Limber pine seeds need an exact amount of soil over them to sprout into new trees. Coincidentally, this is the same depth at which the nutcrackers bury the seeds.

→ THE ALPINE

The alpine zone lies at the very top of Rocky Mountain National Park. It encompasses elevations greater than 11,500 feet (3,505 meters). The alpine is the park's highest and coldest life zone. During the summer, daytime temperatures can reach into the 80°F (27°C) range. But nighttime temperatures can drop into the 40°F (4°C) range.

Alpine winters are brutal. Temperatures are often below 0°F (−18°C) and winds exceed 70 miles per hour (112 kilometers per hour). The alpine receives 40 inches (102 centimeters) of precipitation each year. One half of this comes as snow, but much is lost due to the wind. In some places you'll see huge snowdrifts, and others will be blown completely free of snow.

Furthermore, alpine winters are long. The average temperature on the alpine is below freezing eight months each year. This makes alpine summers too short for trees to grow. The absence of trees makes this life zone easy to identify. The alpine tundra is the land above the trees. This natural boundary is called the tree line or the timberline.

Even the air is thinner. Oxygen is less concentrated here. This "thinner" air makes it difficult for some people to get enough oxygen when they breathe. In addition, more ultraviolet (UV) rays

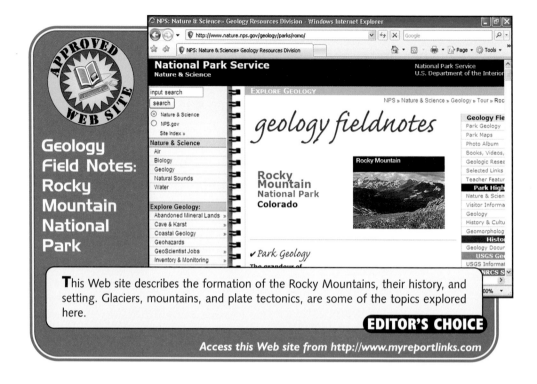

National Park Service
Nature & Science

National Park Service
U.S. Department of the Interior

input search

search

◉ Nature & Science
○ NPS.gov
Site Index »

Nature & Science
Air
Biology
Geology
Natural Sounds
Water

Explore Geology:
Abandoned Mineral Lands »
Cave & Karst »
Coastal Geology »
Geohazards
GeoScientist Jobs »
Inventory & Monitoring »

EXPLORE GEOLOGY

NPS » Nature & Science » Geology » Tour » Roc

geology fieldnotes

Rocky Mountain

Rocky Mountain
National Park
Colorado

✔ *Park Geology*
The grandeur of

Geology Fie
Park Geology
Park Maps
Photo Album
Books, Videos,
Geologic Resea
Selected Links
Teacher Featur
Park High
Nature & Scien
Visitor Informa
Geology
History & Cultu
Geomorpholog
Histo
Geology Docun
USGS Ge
USGS Informat
NRCS S

Geology
Field Notes:
Rocky
Mountain
National
Park

This Web site describes the formation of the Rocky Mountains, their history, and setting. Glaciers, mountains, and plate tectonics, are some of the topics explored here.

EDITOR'S CHOICE

Access this Web site from http://www.myreportlinks.com

come through the atmosphere in the alpine than at sea level.

⮕ TUNDRA

Indeed, the alpine is a harsh environment. Yet, more than two hundred plant species have evolved to live here. This vegetation makes up a part of the alpine called the tundra.

Tundra plants hug the ground to stay warm and out of the wind. All day long, the rocks around them absorb heat from the sun and release it into the air. This is why the air at ground level can be thirty degrees warmer than the air higher up. In addition, many tundra plants contain a chemical—anthocyanin—that helps them convert sunlight to warmth.

Most tundra flowers have waxy leaves and dense tiny hairs. Both protect them from the wind. Many also have long roots that anchor the plants in the windy environment. Grasses and sedges are common tundra plants. Flowers like moss campion, sky pilot, alpine sunflowers, and alpine phlox are plentiful, too.

⊖ ALPINE ANIMALS

Some animals have also adapted to life in the alpine. The yellow-bellied marmot stays here year-round. This marmot has golden-colored fur. It can be 2 feet (61 centimeters) long and weigh up to 11 pounds (5 kilograms).

Marmots make burrows in rocky areas and are frequently seen sunning on rocks. They live in groups of ten to twenty called colonies. Marmots eat grass, leaves, and flowers all summer long to prepare for hibernation during the winter.

Another animal of the alpine is the pika. It is a tiny relative of the rabbit. It looks more like a guinea pig than a rabbit, though. Pikas are grayish brown and grow up to 9 inches (23 centimeters) long. Pikas also live in colonies. They stay active in the winter living off the leaves and grasses they spend all summer gathering. For this reason, the pika is often called the farmer of the tundra.

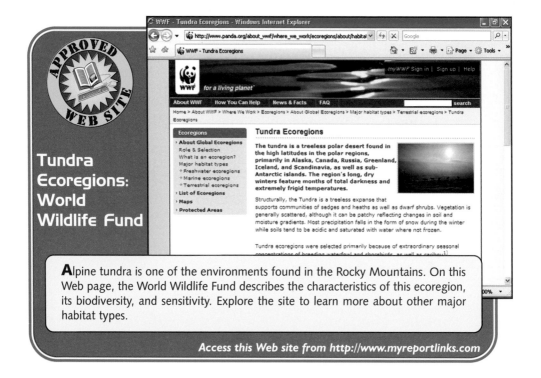

Tundra
Ecoregions:
World
Wildlife Fund

WWF - Tundra Ecoregions - Windows Internet Explorer

http://www.panda.org/about_wwf/where_we_work/ecoregions/about/habitat

WWF - Tundra Ecoregions

myWWF Sign in | Sign up | Help

WWF for a living planet®

About WWF   How You Can Help   News & Facts   FAQ   search

Home > About WWF > Where We Work > Ecoregions > About Global Ecoregions > Major habitat types > Terrestrial ecoregions > Tundra
Ecoregions

Ecoregions
› About Global Ecoregions
  Role & Selection
  What is an ecoregion?
  Major habitat types
    ◆ Freshwater ecoregions
    ◆ Marine ecoregions
    ◆ Terrestrial ecoregions
› List of Ecoregions
› Maps
› Protected Areas

Tundra Ecoregions

The tundra is a treeless polar desert found in the high latitudes in the polar regions, primarily in Alaska, Canada, Russia, Greenland, Iceland, and Scandinavia, as well as sub-Antarctic islands. The region's long, dry winters feature months of total darkness and extremely frigid temperatures.

Structurally, the Tundra is a treeless expanse that supports communities of sedges and heaths as well as dwarf shrubs. Vegetation is generally scattered, although it can be patchy reflecting changes in soil and moisture gradients. Most precipitation falls in the form of snow during the winter while soils tend to be acidic and saturated with water where not frozen.

Tundra ecoregions were selected primarily because of extraordinary seasonal concentrations of breeding waterfowl and shorebirds, as well as caribou.[1]

Alpine tundra is one of the environments found in the Rocky Mountains. On this Web page, the World Wildlife Fund describes the characteristics of this ecoregion, its biodiversity, and sensitivity. Explore the site to learn more about other major habitat types.

Access this Web site from http://www.myreportlinks.com

The white-tailed ptarmigan is the only bird that braves the tundra year-round. At the end of the summer, its mottled brown feathers are replaced with white ones to match the winter snow. The ptarmigan has heavily feathered feet that help it move across the snow.

Ptarmigans are common in the park, yet they are rarely seen because their mottled feathers match the color of the rock. They are masters at sitting still. This makes them hard to spot in their seasonal camouflage.

A few butterflies live on the tundra. They position their wings to face the sun and absorb its heat like tiny solar collectors. Some press themselves against rocks to soak up their heat.

⇒ RIPARIAN

More than 150 lakes and 450 miles of streams lie within the park. They are found in all three life zones. Therefore, each zone has a riparian ecosystem, or one based on water. Riparian plants and animals live in bands around ponds and along streams. The particular species in each environment often depends on the elevation of the water.

One park amphibian lives only at high elevations. The boreal toad is native to Colorado. It makes its home near waters between 8,000 and 12,000 feet (2,438 and 3,658 meters). The boreal toad is about 4 inches (10 centimeters) long and is listed as an endangered species in Colorado and New Mexico.

Seven species of fish are native to Rocky Mountain National Park. Many live throughout the park. One of these is the greenback cutthroat trout. It is named for the red stripes across its jaws. This fish is found only in Colorado.

Greenback cutthroats were once abundant in the park. Their numbers were reduced in the early 1900s by overharvest and habitat destruction. Numbers declined even further when the park's lakes and streams were stocked with nonnative species. For some reason, greenbacks could not compete with the new fish species. By 1937, the greenback was thought to be extinct.[2]

Then, two small populations were discovered north of the park. Various agencies began working to reestablish the fish. Slowly, the greenback began to multiply. Now there is a healthy number in park waters. Several can be spotted from the boardwalk in Hidden Valley.

Below 9,000 feet (2,743 meters), riparian vegetation is diverse. Shrubs such as willows, dogwood, and dwarf birch are common. Aquatic sedge, chiming bells, mountain wood lily, and Canadian reedgrass grow in or near ponds.

▲ There are many layers and ecoregions within RMNP. Some ecoregions or biomes, like the tundra, are home to fewer species than some of the warmer regions.

The fish and amphibians of Rocky Mountain National Park rely on an abundance of insects. Mayflies, dragonflies, and water striders are all common near park steams and lakes.

The Western terrestrial garter snake is the park's only snake. Garters live near streams at lower elevations. They are usually brown and tan with darker spots or stripes. They can grow to more than 3 feet (91 centimeters) in length. Garter snakes can bite, but they are not poisonous.

RIPARIAN MAMMALS

Many riparian mammals are elusive. Beavers are rarely seen, but signs of them are everywhere. Beaver-chewed trees line many streams. Otters, too, are not often seen. But in the winter, their snow slides can be found on slopes near lakes.

About thirty to thirty-five moose live on the park's west side. These 1,000-pound (454-kilogram) animals have antlers that can grow to 6 feet (2 meters) across. Moose are the largest members of the deer family and stand about 6 feet (2 meters) tall at the shoulders. They have long legs, which make them look lanky and awkward. The males have a sac known as a dewlap that hangs beneath their necks. Moose eat willows and water plants. They can be seen in the Kawuneeche Valley on the west side of the park.

BIRDS OF THE RIPARIAN

American dippers are commonly seen feeding in the park's waters. This 6-inch (16-centimeter)-long bird is also known as the water ouzel. It is dark gray with white feathers on the eyelids. Dippers eat water insects and tiny fish. Their name comes from the way they bob their bodies up and down while feeding on the bottom of streams. An extra eyelid allows the dipper to see underwater.

Mallards are also common in the park. These ducks grow to two feet (61 centimeters) long. Males have an iridescent green head and a white neck ring. The rest of the body is brown and light gray. Females are a mottled brown.

BIGHORN SHEEP

Many animals travel between life zones. One is the bighorn sheep. Rocky Mountain bighorn are grayish brown with white lower bodies and rumps. The male sheep, or ram, has horns that curl as they grow. A full-grown curl can be 3 feet (91 centimeters) in length. The female, or ewe, has sharp, straight horns. They grow 10 inches (25 centimeters) long.

Bighorns are designed for life in the mountains. Their hooves are soft and flexible. These act like suction cups against the rock, making bighorns expert jumpers and climbers. Bighorn

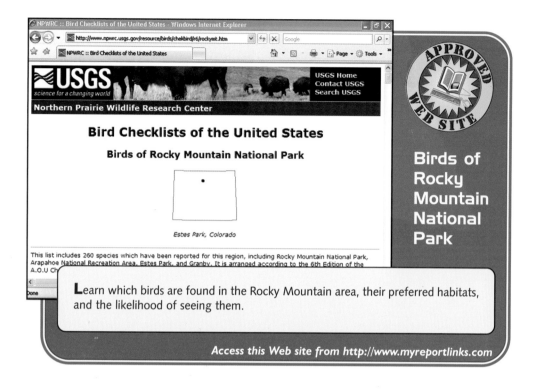

NPWRC :: Bird Checklists of the United States - Windows Internet Explorer

http://www.npwrc.usgs.gov/resource/birds/chekbird/r6/rockymt.htm Google

NPWRC :: Bird Checklists of the United States Page Tools

USGS
science for a changing world

USGS Home
Contact USGS
Search USGS

Northern Prairie Wildlife Research Center

Bird Checklists of the United States

Birds of Rocky Mountain National Park

Estes Park, Colorado

This list includes 260 species which have been reported for this region, including Rocky Mountain National Park, Arapahoe National Recreation Area, Estes Park, and Granby. It is arranged according to the 6th Edition of the A.O.U Ch

Done

Birds of Rocky Mountain National Park

Learn which birds are found in the Rocky Mountain area, their preferred habitats, and the likelihood of seeing them.

Access this Web site from http://www.myreportlinks.com

sheep also have keen eyesight and a sharp sense of smell and hearing. They can detect danger from great distances. This gives them time to escape to rocky crags where predators can't follow.

Bighorn sheep feed on the grasses and small plants of the montane and subalpine. They eat large amounts quickly, then climb high to rechew and digest the food.

There were once thousands of bighorn sheep in the region. However, hunters in the late 1800s shot hundreds for their meat and horns. When ranchers moved to the area, the sheep they brought carried diseases that killed many of the remaining bighorn sheep.

▲ An endangered species, the bighorn sheep is one of the favorites of visitors to RMNP.

Once the area became a park, hunting was prohibited. Ranching also ended. Slowly, bighorn sheep numbers increased. Today, the estimated number of bighorn sheep in the park is about 350, including three herds. Two of the herds, however, (the St. Vrain and Fall River herds) move freely beyond the park's boundaries and are not included in this total number. Most of the bighorn sheep live in groups of five to thirty.

→ ELK

Another Rocky Mountain National Park migrator is the elk. Elk are large animals and can weigh more than 1,000 pounds (454 kilograms). They stand 5 feet (1.5 meters) high at their shoulders. Elk are brown or tan with white on their rumps and tails. They eat grasses, twigs, and shrubs. Male elk are called bulls. Female elk are cows.

Each winter, a bull's antlers shed. They grow back in the summer, in a nutrient-rich sheath of velvet. Their antlers grow up to 1 inch (3 centimeters) a day. The older the bull, the larger the rack of antlers. Mature bulls can have twelve-point racks that weigh 40 pounds (18 kilograms). Some spread more than 5 feet (1.5 meters) across.

During the summer, cows and young bulls live together in herds in the high country. Adult bulls live there, too, either staying alone or living in small groups.

An elk's fur sheds in the late summer. It is replaced with a winter coat of thick coarse hair. This coat is five times warmer than the summer coat. Yet even this is not enough to keep the elk warm during an alpine winter. So as summer wanes and the nights grow chilly, elk head to lower elevations.

September marks the beginning of the elk rut. This is the breeding season. During the rut, the bulls compete for the right to mate with the

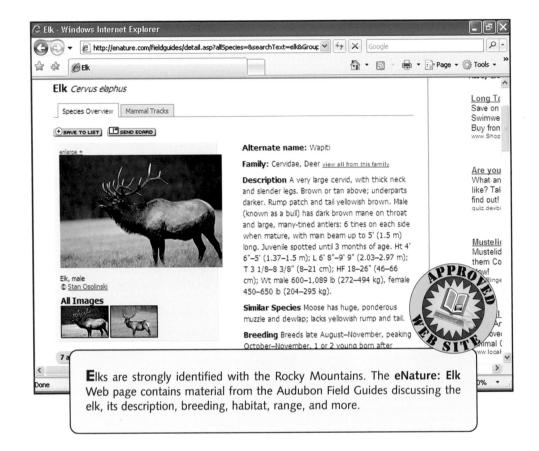

Elk *Cervus elaphus*

Species Overview | Mammal Tracks

SAVE TO LIST | SEND ECARD

enlarge +

Elk, male
© Stan Osolinski

All Images

Alternate name: Wapiti

Family: Cervidae, Deer view all from this family

Description A very large cervid, with thick neck and slender legs. Brown or tan above; underparts darker. Rump patch and tail yellowish brown. Male (known as a bull) has dark brown mane on throat and large, many-tined antlers: 6 tines on each side when mature, with main beam up to 5' (1.5 m) long. Juvenile spotted until 3 months of age. Ht 4' 6"–5' (1.37–1.5 m); L 6' 8"–9' 9" (2.03–2.97 m); T 3 1/8–8 3/8" (8–21 cm); HF 18–26" (46–66 cm); Wt male 600–1,089 lb (272–494 kg), female 450–650 lb (204–295 kg).

Similar Species Moose has huge, ponderous muzzle and dewlap; lacks yellowish rump and tail.

Breeding Breeds late August–November, peaking October–November. 1 or 2 young born after

Elks are strongly identified with the Rocky Mountains. The **eNature: Elk** Web page contains material from the Audubon Field Guides discussing the elk, its description, breeding, habitat, range, and more.

females, or cows. Once a bull moves into a herd of cows, he is said to have a harem. An average harem is around a dozen.

Bulls proclaim ownership of a harem by bugling. An elk bugle starts as a low groan, then turns into a shrill squeal or whine. Bugling can also attract more cows.

⊕ BATTLING BULLS

In fact, cows often leave one harem for another. Bulls, therefore, watch their harems constantly, circling and guarding their cows to keep them from straying. Conflicts arise when a bull tries to steal a cow from another bull's harem. These showdowns start with the two bulls trotting toward each other with their heads held high. When neither bull retreats, a battle begins.

Antlers clack as bulls push against each other, trying to knock the other off balance. Then the bulls break loose. Sometimes the weaker bull trots off in defeat. Sometimes the two go at it again. Bulls rarely fight to the death.

As the breeding season ends, cows and bulls separate. Cows move off to winter in herds. Bulls often stay together, too.

➲ RAPTORS

Many raptors, birds that hunt for food using their talons, inhabit the park. They have a curved tip to their beak. Raptor numbers declined all across the nation beginning in the 1960s. Loss of habitat, pesticide use, and hunting all greatly reduced the number of raptors. Laws passed during the following years helped most species recover. Today Rocky Mountain National Park provides a safe habitat for many of these birds.

Red-tailed hawks are the most commonly seen raptors in the park. They prefer the montane zone. They are the largest hawk at 26 inches (66

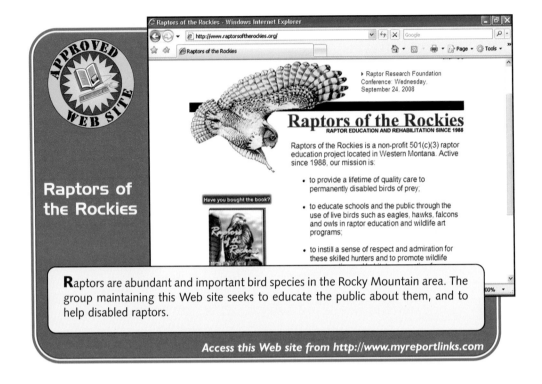

Raptors of the Rockies - Windows Internet Explorer

http://www.raptorsoftherockies.org/

Raptors of the Rockies

▸ Raptor Research Foundation
Conference: Wednesday,
September 24, 2008

Raptors of the Rockies
RAPTOR EDUCATION AND REHABILITATION SINCE 1988

Raptors of the Rockies is a non-profit 501(c)(3) raptor
education project located in Western Montana. Active
since 1988, our mission is:

- to provide a lifetime of quality care to
  permanently disabled birds of prey;

- to educate schools and the public through the
  use of live birds such as eagles, hawks, falcons
  and owls in raptor education and wildlife art
  programs;

- to instill a sense of respect and admiration for
  these skilled hunters and to promote wildlife

Have you bought the book?

Raptors of the Rockies

Raptors are abundant and important bird species in the Rocky Mountain area. The
group maintaining this Web site seeks to educate the public about them, and to
help disabled raptors.

Access this Web site from http://www.myreportlinks.com

centimeters) and have rounded red tails. Red-
tailed hawks eat rodents, birds, and snakes.

Golden eagles also live in the park. They can be
40 inches (102 centimeters) long, with wingspans
that stretch to 7 feet (2.1 meters). They are dark
brown with a light gold color on the backs of their
necks. Golden eagles prey on yellow-bellied marmots, squirrels, rabbits, and birds. They usually
take prey on the ground from a low flight, but are
able to grab birds in flight. Sometimes, golden
eagles hunt in pairs.

Peregrine falcons live in the park, too. Peregrines have a wingspan of 3 feet (91 centimeters).
Their backs and wings are blue gray with light

gray or white faces and necks. Peregrines are one of the world's fastest birds. They can dive at speeds of 87 miles per hour (140 kilometers per hour).

The great horned owl is another park raptor. It is the largest tufted owl in North America. The great horned owl is 25 inches (63 centimeters) tall and has a wingspan 5 feet (1.5 meters) long. These night-flying birds nest in ponderosa pines and are more often heard than seen.

The northern pygmy-owl lives in the montane forests of the park. Yet it is also seen as high as 12,000 feet (3,658 meters). This little owl only grows to about 6 inches (15 centimeters). The northern pygmy has a brown and white body with a long narrow tail. It eats mice, birds, and even large insects.

Including raptors, about 280 different kinds of birds have been sighted in the park. Many of them, such as the white-tailed ptarmigan, Clark's nutcracker, mountain chickadee, American dipper, and western tanager are unique to mountainous habitats.[3] Because of this, Rocky Mountain National Park has been named a global Important Bird Area (IBA). This means the area is vital to the continuation of certain bird species.[4]

5

Elk are overpopulated in Rocky Mountain National Park. Officials are looking to take steps to cut back the number of elk in the park.

Challenges to the Park

When the National Park Service was founded in 1916, part of its purpose was to help the parks "conserve the scenery and the natural and historic objects and the wild life therein . . . by such means as will leave them unimpaired for the enjoyment of future generations."[1] This has become more of a challenge with each passing year. Today, many problems face Rocky Mountain National Park.

⇒ ELK

One of the park's biggest problems is an overpopulation of elk. There are now more than three thousand elk in the park. Yet the vegetation in the park cannot support this many elk. Park meadows are overgrazed, leaving less vegetation for other animals. In addition, overgrazed meadows force elk to eat aspen. This makes fewer homes for cavity nesting birds and other animals that live among the aspen.

The high number of elk also causes problems with people in Estes Park. Nearly two thousand elk winter in or near the town. They frequently wander onto highways or destroy lawns and gardens.

Park officials want all of the park's animals and plants to have a place in the ecosystem for years to come. After careful study, many scientists believe that elk numbers should be reduced to achieve a healthy balance in the ecosystem. Officials have considered bringing wolves, a natural elk predator, into the park. They have also considered various control measures, such as moving elk to other places, fencing certain areas, and hunting outside the park boundaries.

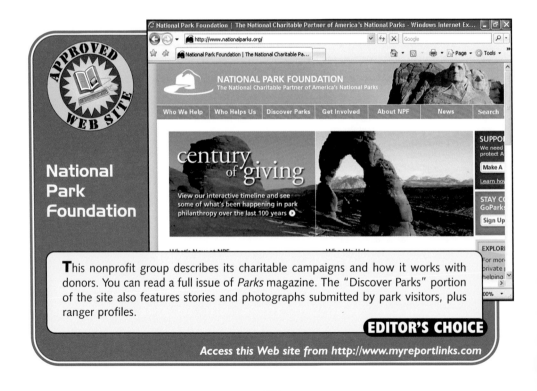

National Park Foundation

This nonprofit group describes its charitable campaigns and how it works with donors. You can read a full issue of *Parks* magazine. The "Discover Parks" portion of the site also features stories and photographs submitted by park visitors, plus ranger profiles.

EDITOR'S CHOICE

Access this Web site from http://www.myreportlinks.com

In 2007, park officials drafted a plan to cull the elk. That is, to reduce the number of elk. However, the method of culling and number of elk that may be culled have yet to be decided. Parts of the park would be closed to visitors while the culling is taking place.[2] The park must have permission from Congress before culling takes place. As of this writing, Congress is still considering the plan.

→ CHRONIC WASTING DISEASE

Another animal issue is chronic wasting disease (CWD). CWD is a fatal neurological disease that affects both the deer and elk populations in the park. Left untreated, CWD could drastically reduce the park's entire deer population.

Officials hope to halt the disease before it spreads. To do this, infected animals must be killed. Deer are regularly captured so a small tissue sample can be taken from their mouths. Samples are tested for CWD.

Uninfected deer are given an ear tag and radio collar and set free. This allows wildlife officials to track the deer for future research. Sick animals are euthanized so they won't spread the disease.

→ SPECIES INVASION

Another problem in the park is the invasion of nonnative plants, or plants that do not naturally occur in a region. Seeds from nonnatives come into the park on wind, water, shoes, and even car tires. Some of these seeds sprout and grow in their new home.

About 120 park plants are nonnative. Twelve of these are considered noxious weeds. Noxious weeds are weeds that choke out native plants. They spread quickly, taking over large areas of land. Most noxious weeds have no food value. Some are even poisonous to animals.

Rocky Mountain National Park's worst weed is the leafy spurge. This yellowish green plant has heart-shaped leaves and can grow to 4 feet (1 meter) tall. Spurge spreads by seed and root. It destroys all nearby plants and takes over entire meadows. Other noxious weeds in the park include musk thistle and yellow toadflax.

Officials use several methods to control noxious weeds. They pull them, introduce insects that feed on them, and even use chemicals to stop the plants from spreading.

⊜ CLIMATE CHANGE

How is global climate change affecting Rocky Mountain National Park? Scientists have already noticed changes in park life due to a changing climate.

One such change is a recent outbreak in bark beetle infestation. While in the past this has been a cyclical problem occurring every ten to thirty years, it seems to have worsened in the last few years. Many experts think this is a result of rising temperatures which brought on an extended drought.[3] Infected trees are removed and burned. Insecticides are sprayed on trees near camp-grounds and picnic areas to prevent them from becoming infected.

Scientists expect to see other changes due to a warming climate. For example, warming will change the park vegetation. Fewer wildflowers will grow in montane meadows. Experts estimate that for each degree of global warming, the tree

 Some scientists blame climate change, or global warming, on the increased number of bark beetles wreaking havoc in the park. You can see how bark beetles have eaten away much of the bark of this tree.

line will encroach on the tundra by about 250 feet (76 meters). This will create different vegetation at the mountaintops; it is thought that a five degree rise in temperature could eliminate half of the park's alpine tundra.[4]

A warmer climate could also reduce the amount of snowfall the park receives.[5] Ptarmigans are one species that could be greatly affected by a loss of snow. They build snow caves to keep from freezing in the winter. They also use snowpacks as ladders to reach willow shrub branches for food.

Ptarmigans are already reacting to earlier springs by hatching earlier. This leaves babies vulnerable to the low food supplies of the alpine winters. In just twenty years, the birds' numbers have been cut in half. Some experts predict that if global warming continues the birds could be extinct by the middle of the century. Other animals of the alpine may face similar problems.[6]

BUTTERFLIES

Scientists are looking at how climate changes might be affecting other park life. One project has scientists examining global warming and its effect on butterflies.

Butterflies are very sensitive to climate change. Warming can cause a shift in the areas where they live and even reduce their numbers. Therefore, a

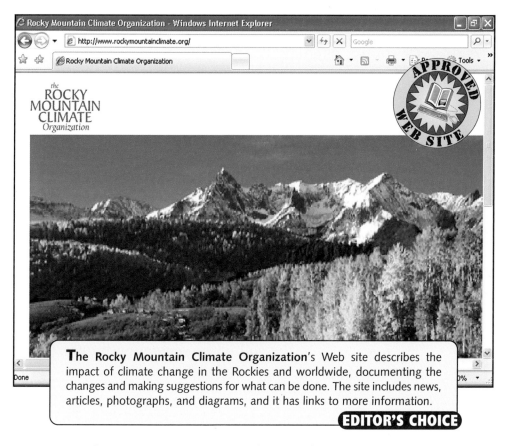

The **Rocky Mountain Climate Organization**'s Web site describes the impact of climate change in the Rockies and worldwide, documenting the changes and making suggestions for what can be done. The site includes news, articles, photographs, and diagrams, and it has links to more information.

EDITOR'S CHOICE

change in the number of butterflies in an area can be a sign of a changing climate.

More than 125 species of butterflies inhabit the park. Each week for several years, volunteers have been counting butterflies in certain areas. Although it is still too soon to draw solid conclusions, researchers have noticed that the numbers of cold-climate butterflies in the area have declined.[7]

Finally, a warmer climate will lead to drier summers and longer droughts. This could result in more lightning-caused wildfires.

FIRE

Of course, lightning doesn't always set off forest fires; careless people can start fires, too. Fires kill wildlife and destroy animal habitat and food. Some fires grow so large that they threaten human lives and property.

Yet some fires can also be beneficial. They clear overcrowded trees. Thinned forests are better at fighting off insects and disease. Fires also clear the forests of deadwood and layers of pine needles. This reduces the amount of fuel available when fires break out.

Fires can be helpful in other ways. Nutrients are released into the soil when vegetation burns, and this helps to feed new plants. Finally, some species such as lodgepole pine need fire in order to make new plants.

After a fire, different plants grow in a burned area than were there before. These new plants create food and habitat for different types of animals. Therefore, fires encourage diversity in an ecosystem.

Park officials manage fires carefully. Small fires are seen as healthy. When they are contained, most fires are allowed to burn themselves out. Rangers even set small fires under carefully controlled circumstances to clear dead wood.

However, dry and windy conditions can turn small fires into life- and property-threatening events. So all fires are closely monitored. During

The painted lady butterfly is one of over 125 butterfly species found in RMNP.

dry weather, camp-fires and outdoor grilling are prohibited. And any fires that threaten to grow out of control are put out as quickly as possible.

➯ POLLUTION

Rocky Mountain National Park streams and lakes are crystal clear. Yet giardia, a microscopic organism, is found in park waters. Giardia comes into the water from animal and human waste. When ingested, giardia can cause diarrhea, cramps, bloating, and weight loss. Visitors should never drink directly from a park stream or lake.

There are other kinds of pollution in the park. Some comes from cars, while nearby industries and power plants also emit pollutants. All of these emissions can create haze. Not only does this reduce visibility, it affects people's health. People with asthma, emphysema, and other breathing problems are most effected.

In addition, pollutants find their way into park water and soil. Currently, nitrogen oxides are

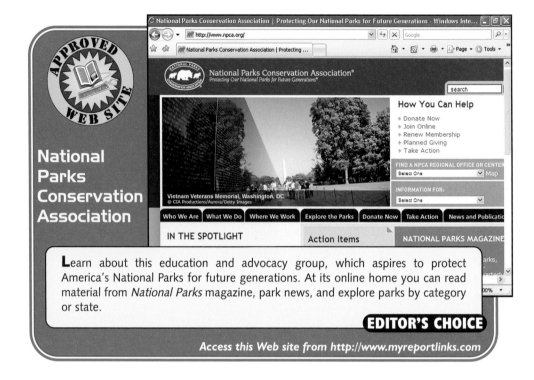

National Parks Conservation Association

National Parks Conservation Association®
Protecting Our National Parks for Future Generations®

search

How You Can Help
→ Donate Now
→ Join Online
→ Renew Membership
→ Planned Giving
→ Take Action

FIND A NPCA REGIONAL OFFICE OR CENTER
Select One   Map

INFORMATION FOR:
Select One

Vietnam Veterans Memorial, Washington, DC
© CIA Productions/Aurora/Getty Images

Who We Are | What We Do | Where We Work | Explore the Parks | Donate Now | Take Action | News and Publicatio

IN THE SPOTLIGHT   Action Items   NATIONAL PARKS MAGAZINE

Learn about this education and advocacy group, which aspires to protect America's National Parks for future generations. At its online home you can read material from *National Parks* magazine, park news, and explore parks by category or state.

EDITOR'S CHOICE

Access this Web site from http://www.myreportlinks.com

causing the most damage. They come from car and factory emissions. In addition, nearby farms use nitrogen fertilizers. Some of this nitrogen also finds its way into the park.

Nitrogen pollution makes park soil and water acidic. The amount of nitrogen in the park's water is now fifteen to twenty times higher than natural levels.[8] Many plants and animals cannot live in soil or water that is too acidic.

The effects of this have already been seen. Some plants are dying and others are taking their place. Nitrogen has also changed the chemistry in spruce trees, making them more susceptible to insects, drought, and cold.[9]

Experts are working to combat pollution. Park rangers encourage visitors to travel on the free shuttle buses inside the park. This reduces the number of cars on park roads. In addition, activists are working for laws that limit toxic emissions from area farms and factories.

→ HUMAN USE

Rocky Mountain National Park attracts millions of visitors each year. Every one impacts the park, and some do lasting damage. So park officials work to balance the needs of the natural environment with the public's desire to experience the park fully.

The park's tundra is especially fragile. A 4-inch (10-centimeter) plant might be fifty years old. Therefore, a few footsteps on the tundra can destroy centuries of growth. So the park has built trails that go out into the tundra. This allows people to experience the land without destroying it.

In addition, many people come to the park to see the wildlife. Yet excited visitors can hurt the wildlife. For instance, people eager to see bighorn sheep often get too close, and this stresses the sensitive animals. Stress makes bighorns more likely to become sick. In fact, human-caused stress is the largest factor limiting the growth of the park's bighorn populations.

Some tourists enjoy feeding chipmunks, magpies, and other animals. While tourists are a

▲ This Clark's nutcracker is perched on a branch of a pine tree. Some park visitors don't realize that feeding animals such as the Clark's nutcracker can disrupt the gentle balance of the park's wildlife.

plentiful source of food in the summer, few are around in the winter. Human snacks are not part of the natural diet of wild animals, and eating them can weaken their immune systems and chances for survival. The animals that have been fed by humans do not know how to find their own food during the cold months. Many starve during that time, while others become so weak they are easy prey.

Furthermore, feeding animals can disrupt the natural balance of an ecosystem. For instance, feeding Clark's nutcrackers reduces the number of limber pine seeds that are buried. This reduces the number of new trees that sprout.

Even the most respectful visitors may disturb or harm wildlife without knowing it. Climbers seeking challenging routes sometimes disturb raptors nesting in high cliffs. When climbers compete with wildlife for territory, park officials rule for the wildlife. Certain climbing routes and hiking trails are closed during the spring. This gives raptors nesting privacy.

⮕ PEOPLE IN TROUBLE

Each year illness, injury, and even death result from lack of preparedness in the mountains. Mountain visits require preparation. First, the body must adjust to higher elevations; this takes time. People from lower altitudes need to spend a few days in the area before attempting any physically demanding activity. Its symptoms include nausea, headaches, and shortness of breath. People who experience altitude sickness should move to lower elevations.

Hypothermia is another condition that can affect park visitors. Hypothermia occurs when the body temperature drops too low for muscle and brain activities. It is often brought on by exposure to wet and cold. Hypothermia can be fatal. People with hypothermia may feel sleepy and cannot stop shivering. A person with hypothermia should be warmed with dry clothing and warm liquids.

Dressing in layers and carrying a windproof shell prepares visitors for Rocky Mountain National Park's changeable weather. Furthermore, visitors should wear sunglasses, sunscreen, and a hat to protect themselves from strong UV rays and sunburn.

Another mountain danger is the lightning storm. Lightning strikes quite often during afternoon thunderstorms. Visitors should take lightning seriously and follow appropriate precautions. One of these is to begin hikes early and descend from high mountains by early afternoon.

Search and rescue teams go out each year to find lost or injured visitors. Even careful visitors can have accidents. Therefore, hikers and climbers should not travel alone. They should always tell someone where they are headed and when they will return.

FUNDING

One of the biggest problems in all of the national parks is money. Although park costs have risen in recent years, budgets have not kept up. Some experts estimate that the National Park Service's annual budget is $600 million dollars short of what the parks actually need.[10] Lack of adequate funds has meant a cut in park services and

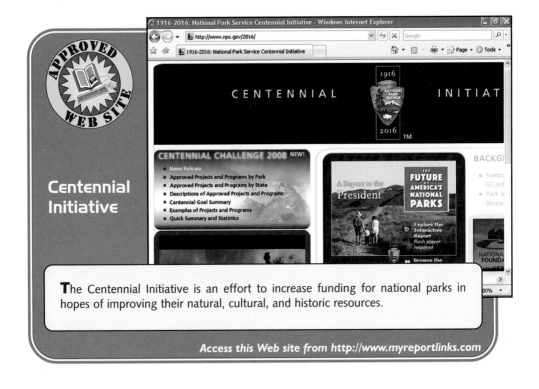

Centennial Initiative

The Centennial Initiative is an effort to increase funding for national parks in hopes of improving their natural, cultural, and historic resources.

Access this Web site from http://www.myreportlinks.com

programs. Some parks have had to cut ranger staffs, services, and even visitor center hours.

At Rocky Mountain National Park, Lily Lake Visitor Center has been closed due to budget constraints.[11] Public education programs have also been reduced.[12]

In 2006, President George W. Bush announced a program that would increase funding to the national parks. The Centennial Initiative calls for the federal government to match private donations to the national parks. This is an effort to improve park facilities and lands for the one hundredth anniversary of the National Park Service in 2016.[13]

Chapter

6

There are over 350 miles of hiking trails in Rocky Mountain National Park. One of the them is Bear Lake Trail, shown here.

What First?

In 2006, Rocky Mountain National Park was one of the top ten most visited national parks in the United States.[1] Most people come in the summer, yet other seasons are just as appealing. Autumn brings the elk rut set against golden aspen and sharp blue skies. Winter descends on the park with stillness and snow. Spring features waterfalls born of melting snows and new life sprouting everywhere. A visit to Rocky Mountain National Park during any season is a wonderful experience.

➡ DAY TRIPS

Many people come to the park for a scenic drive. There are only a few roads in the park. Yet each one offers breathtaking views. Pullouts scattered along them make good picnic spots.

One of the most popular summer drives is a loop that starts in Horseshoe

Park. Drivers make the slow climb up the Old Fall River Road. After enjoying the sites at the top, visitors drive down Trail Ridge Road. This route includes plenty of "ear popping" as the elevation changes some 4,000 feet (1,219 meters) each way.

There is a good probability of seeing wildlife at any time of the year, even from a car. Elk can be seen in the high country in the summer and in the lower valleys in the winter. Mule deer, elk, moose, and coyotes can be seen year-round. Birds are ever-present, and in the summer, chipmunks and squirrels are everywhere.

The fall elk rut attracts hundreds of people to the park each September. For more than a month, this mating ritual can be seen at dawn and dusk all over the park. The best viewing sites are in Moraine Park, Horseshoe Park, and the Kawuneeche Valley.

The night sky over Rocky Mountain National Park provides an excellent place to watch the stars. Constellations are almost always visible. Each August the Perseids meteor shower brings stargazers from near and far hoping to "catch" a falling star.

HIKING

Rocky Mountain National Park has more than 350 miles (563 kilometers) of hiking trails. From level mile loops around mountain lakes to high-altitude climbing, every visitor will find a hike to enjoy. There are also trails that are wheelchair accessible. Two of the most popular short and level hikes are the trails around Bear Lake and Sprague Lake.

One of the park's most challenging trails is the one to the top of Longs Peak. This 8-mile (12-kilometer) climb goes from 9,000 to 14,259 feet (2,743 to 4,346 meters). Hikers should be in

▲ These park visitors are enjoying a nature hike.

excellent physical condition before attempting the mountain. It is a rigorous hike even for the well trained. In fact, more than fifty climbers have died trying to climb Longs Peak.[2]

There are other trails that climbers can enjoy. Hallett Peak and Lumpy Ridge offer several technical routes. This kind of climbing requires ropes and plenty of expertise. Those who tackle long hikes and climbs should be ready for any kind of weather. Sunny summer mornings can change suddenly into afternoon thunderstorms.

A horseback ride is another way to see the park. More than 200 miles (322 kilometers) of park trails are open to horses. Livery stables in and around the park have horses for any level of rider.

⮕ FISHING

Fly fishing is another popular pastime in the park. Fishing requires a license and some park waters are off limits to anglers. Others are catch and release. Fish caught in these lakes and streams must be returned to the water. This practice keeps the fish population growing. Fishermen should be aware of park regulations before casting their lines into any water.

⮕ CAMPING

For many people, Rocky Mountain National Park has too much to see and do in one day. Those who

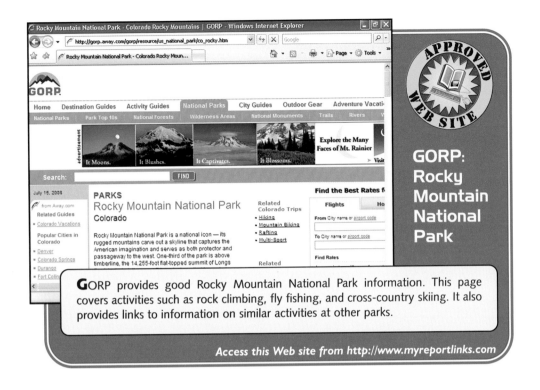

GORP:
Rocky
Mountain
National
Park

GORP provides good Rocky Mountain National Park information. This page covers activities such as rock climbing, fly fishing, and cross-country skiing. It also provides links to information on similar activities at other parks.

Access this Web site from http://www.myreportlinks.com

want to experience the park fully camp in one of its five campgrounds. Each one has its own charm. In addition, there are handicapped-accessible camps and group camps. A few campgrounds are even open in the winter. The park's campgrounds fill up early each day between June and August, and reservations are recommended.

Many people combine hiking and camping by backpacking. They pack everything they need onto their backs, then hike into the wilderness for a few nights. One of the most popular backpacking areas is Wild Basin on the east side of the park. It is enjoyed for its rugged wildness. All visiting backpackers must obtain a permit before heading into the wilderness.

⇒ WINTER ACTIVITIES

The park has plenty of winter fans, too. During the winter, the crowds are gone and the park is quiet. Snow blankets the alpine and subalpine. Although cold and high winds are always possible, mild temperatures are frequent in the montane and lower subalpine zones. Properly dressed visitors can enjoy a variety of winter sports under a bright blue sky.

Trails on the west side are almost always covered with snow. This makes them excellent for cross-country skiing. Adams Falls is a popular destination. Its frozen waters create an almost magical site.

On the east side, snow cover is less consistent. Certain trails are great for skiing, while others are better for snowshoeing. Bear Lake offers a variety of trails for both.

Those wanting to sled can visit Hidden Valley. A small warming house there is a cozy place to rest and refuel.

Winter trekkers must be careful of avalanches. The risk is greatest in steep gullies below snowy slopes. Avalanches of snow on slopes steeper than thirty to forty-five degrees can be easily triggered. People traveling in these areas should wear

WebRangers

The online version of the Junior Rangers program has educational activities, a scavenger hunt, and Web cams from national parks. Each activity has links to relevant Web pages. Register to get your own "virtual Ranger Station," where you can track your progress in completing the WebRanger program.

Access this Web site from http://www.myreportlinks.com

electronic transceivers and know how to use them in case of an avalanche.

Finally, many lower trails on the eastern side are dry during much of the winter and can be hiked. Winter hiking is quiet and uncrowded and wildlife is often seen.

EDUCATION

A trip to Rocky Mountain National Park offers many learning opportunities. Free ranger talks explain a number of topics and are usually held in the living laboratory of the park. On summer nights, many talks are presented at campground amphitheaters by park rangers.

Several historic park buildings now house museums. Some are even listed in the National Register of Historic Places. To be eligible for this, a building must be important to the nation's history in some way. For example, the Holzarth Ranch is in the register because of its early link to ranching and tourism.

THE PARK AS LABORATORY

Many organizations conduct research in the park. Biologists study the park's plant and animal life. Archaeologists search for clues about how people used the park in prehistoric times. Environmental scientists study the effects of climate change on park ecosystems.

In addition, an Artist-in-Residence Program lets artists practice their craft inside the park. Selected artists live in a park cabin for a week while creating a work related to the park. Photographers, writers, and painters all make use of this program.

ESTES PARK

Estes Park is the eastern gateway to Rocky Mountain National Park. Its main street is lined with shops. They offer an array of goods from T-shirts to fine American Indian art. This is a friendly town for tourists with family activities. Among them are miniature golf and go-carting. In addition, Estes Park hosts several festivals each year. Two of the most popular are summer's Rooftop Rodeo and autumn's Elk Fest.

A number of outfitters in Estes Park specialize in helping people enjoy the mountains. They provide equipment, lessons, and even guided trips for hiking, snowshoeing, and horseback riding.

Estes Park offers a variety of restaurants and hotels. Tourists looking for a memorable place to stay might like the historic Stanley Hotel. This building was the inspiration for the haunted hotel in Stephen King's 1977 book, *The Shining*, which was later made into a blockbuster film.

Estes Park is also home to historic buildings related to the park. For instance, the original frame building that housed the park's first headquarters is now behind the Estes Park Museum. And Enos Mills's log cabin is located a short drive out of town.

GRAND LAKE

Grand Lake lies on the west side of the park. It is a smaller town, but it also caters to tourists. Its history is steeped in the lore of the Wild West. American Indian battles, saloons, and shoot-outs all played a role in the town's early days. Today, Grand Lake still has a bit of this Old West flavor. Grand Lake also has many restaurants and shops.

Here, too, a variety of town outfitters can prepare tourists for almost any outdoor activity.

In addition, Grand Lake offers a number of lodging possibilities. The most picturesque is Grand Lake Lodge. It was built just outside the park in the late 1910s. The main building is made of lodgepole pine. Its restaurant and front porch overlook the lake. Cabins in the forest behind the lodge house guests.

CAREERS

Many people who visit Rocky Mountain National Park never leave. Some open businesses or work in the nearby towns. Others join the ranks of National Park Service employees.

The park hires all kinds of specialists. Scientists, firefighters, educators, engineers, naturalists, and even archaeologists are all needed in the park. From its first staff of three rangers, today's park staff has grown to nearly two hundred. In addition, more than two thousand people volunteer in the park each year. All park workers are vigilant about protecting the land and preserving the park for future generations. They are also committed to giving today's tourists an unforgettable experience.

Lucky visitors to Rocky Mountain National Park will see the alpenglow. This phenomenon occurs when the setting sun reflects off of snow

▲ *Some people are so taken with the scenic beauty of Rocky Mountain National Park that they move to the area so they can work there.*

to make the mountain peaks glow red and orange. But those who miss nature's fireworks can experience another kind of alpenglow. This one comes from a quiet walk across a mountain meadow or a stroll through a fragrant forest. These create an alpenglow, too—an alpenglow of the spirit.

Report Links

The Internet sites described below can be accessed at http://www.myreportlinks.com

▶**National Park Service: Rocky Mountain National Park**
Editor's Choice The official Web site of Rocky Mountain National Park.

▶**Rocky Mountain National Park Virtual Tour**
Editor's Choice Take a photo tour of Rocky Mountain National Park.

▶**National Parks Conservation Association**
Editor's Choice The NPCA helps maintain and protect America's national parks.

▶**National Park Foundation**
Editor's Choice Learn about America's national parks and how you can aid them.

▶**Geology Field Notes: Rocky Mountain National Park**
Editor's Choice Find out how the Rocky Mountains were formed.

▶**The Rocky Mountain Climate Organization**
Editor's Choice See how climate change has affected the Rockies and what can be done about it.

▶**About.com: International Biosphere Reserves**
Discover why Rocky Mountain National Park has been named an International Biosphere Reserve.

▶**America's Volcanic Past: Rocky Mountains**
Learn about the influence of volcanoes in the formation of the Rocky Mountain area.

▶**Birds of Rocky Mountain National Park**
Get to know the birds of the Rocky Mountain area.

▶**Centennial Initiative**
Read about a partnership to improve America's national parks in time for their hundred-year anniversary.

▶**eNature: Elk**
Learn all about elk, a common sight in the Rocky Mountains.

▶**Enos Mills Cabin Museum & Gallery**
Get to know the man who has been referred to as the "Father of Rocky Mountain Park."

▶**Geologic Time: The Story of a Changing Earth**
The Smithsonian Institute has posted this Web page about the formation of the earth's crust.

▶**GORP: Rocky Mountain National Park**
Using this Web site, you can plan a visit to RMNP centered on outdoor activities.

▶**HowStuffWorks: Rocky Mountain National Park**
Review the natural history of the Rocky Mountains and explore its sightseeing opportunities.

MyReportLinks.com Books

Report Links

The Internet sites described below can be accessed at http://www.myreportlinks.com

▶**Important Bird Areas Program**
Learn about the Audubon Society's Important Bird Area program and its other activities.

▶**John Wesley Powell Memorial Museum**
The life and times of one of the early explorers of the Rocky Mountains area, John Wesley Powell.

▶**Kawuneeche Valley Holzwarth Historic Site**
Get a closer look at a dude ranch in the Rocky Mountains that dates to the 1920s.

▶***National Geographic*: Rocky Mountain National Park**
Explore RMNP and nearby forests, monuments, and wildlife refuges.

▶**National Park Service**
The official Web site of the National Park Service, part of the U.S. Dept. of the Interior.

▶**Oh Ranger!: Rocky Mountain National Park**
Gather info about Rocky Mountain National Park and other U.S. parks on this Web site.

▶**Perry-Castañeda Library Map Collection: Maps of United States National Parks**
View this collection of national park maps provided by the University of Texas Libraries.

▶**Raptors of the Rockies**
This nonprofit group helps injured birds of prey in the Rocky Mountain area.

▶**Rocky Mountain National Park**
Use this Web site to plan an activity-oriented trip to Rocky Mountain.

▶**Rocky Mountain Nature Association**
Download the Rocky Mountain Nature Association's newspaper-format guide to the park.

▶**Roosevelt's Tree Army**
See how the CCC helped expand and maintain America's national parks in the 1930s.

▶**Tundra Ecoregions: World Wildlife Fund**
Learn all about alpine tundra and the importance of this ecoregion.

▶**UNESCO: Biosphere Reserves**
Find out about the UN International Biosphere Reserves program, and why RMNP is part of it.

▶**U.S. Forest Service: Rocky Mountain Region**
Learn about forests, forest management, and conservation in the Rocky Mountain region at this site.

▶**WebRangers**
Can't make it to a national park? The WebRangers program is the next best thing to being there!

alluvial fan—A fan-shaped area of rock and plant deposits made by flowing water.

alpine—Land in the mountains that is above the tree line.

climate change—Changes in modern climate including the rise in temperatures often referred to as global warming.

Continental Divide—A line of elevated land that forms a division. Water on one side of the divide runs to one ocean and water on the other side runs to another.

cull—The selection and removal of certain animals from surplus stock. The removal may be by killing or relocation.

euthanize—To put something to death or let something die in a painless way.

giardia—A parasite that causes infection in a person's gastrointestinal system.

glacier—A large field of ice made from layers of snow.

gneiss—A gray metamorphic rock found in Rocky Mountains National Park.

Great Depression—A decline in the world economy beginning in 1929 and lasting until 1939. During the Great Depression many Americans were unemployed and lived in poverty.

hypothermia—A condition in which a person's body temperature drops lower than is needed for normal function.

iridescent—A rainbow of colors caused by the refraction of light.

krummholz—An area of trees near the tree line with twisted branches caused by constant wind.

montane—An area of mountainous land below subalpine elevations characterized by distinctive plant and animal life.

mountain range—A group of mountains bordered by lowlands, passes, or rivers.

native—Something that occurs in an area naturally or has been there for a long time (plants, animals, people).

noxious weeds—Plants that are damaging to other plants, animals, or humans.

park—A broad level valley between mountains.

riparian—Relating to rivers and lakes.

schist—A metamorphic rock found in Rocky Mountain National Park that features parallel lines throughout its surface.

snowpack—A buildup of frozen ice and snow.

subalpine—An area of land in the mountains below the tree line and above the montane. The subalpine zone is characterized by distinctive plant and animal life.

technical climbing—Climbing rocks and cliffs using safety equipment and ropes.

timberline—The elevation at which trees can no longer grow due to environmental conditions.

tree line—See timberline.

tundra—An area of land where plants are short because the climate is too cold and harsh for trees to grow.

uplift—A geologic process in which pieces of the earth collide and force land upward.

Chapter 1. The View From the Top

1. John Boslough, *America's National Parks* (Lincolnwood, Ill.: Publications International, 1990), p. 235.

2. National Park Service, "Road Conditions and Closures," *Rocky Mountain National Park,* June 12, 2007, <http://www.nps.gov/romo/planyourvisit/trail_ridge_road_const.htm> (July 3, 2007).

3. National Park Service, "Weather and Climate," *Rocky Mountain National Park, n.d.,* <http://www.nps.gov/romo/visit/weather/weatherandclimate.html> (September 25, 2008).

4. Health and Science, "Ten Most Visited National Parks, 2005," *InfoPlease,* n.d., <http://www.infoplease.com/ipa/A0004743.html> (July 3, 2007).

Chapter 2. Before There Was a Park

1. National Park Service, "Geologic Activity: Glaciers and Geology," *Rocky Mountain National Park,* October 18, 2007, <http://www.nps.gov/romo/naturescience/geologicactivity.htm> (July 15, 2008).

2. Associated Press, "Scientists Surprised to Find New Glaciers in Rocky Mountain Park," *The Olympian,* October 5, 2001, <http://news.theolympian.com/outdoors/environment/119446.shtml> (July 3, 2007).

3. Dougald MacDonald, *Longs Peak: The Story of Colorado's Favorite Fourteener* (Englewood, Colo.: Westcliffe Publishers, 2004), p. 55.

4. Isabella Bird, *A Lady's Life in the Rocky Mountains* (Norman: University of Oklahoma Press, 1960), p. 54.

5. James H. Pickering, *America's Switzerland* (Boulder: University Press of Colorado, 2005), p. 17.

6. National Park Service, "Elk," *Rocky Mountain National Park,* n.d., <http://www.nps.gov/romo/naturescience/elk.htm> (July 3, 2007).

7. Pickering, p. 102.

8. Alexander Drummond, *Enos Mills: Citizen of Nature* (Niwot: University Press of Colorado, 1995), p. 377.

9. Pickering, p. 11.

Chapter 3. The New Park

1. "Perilous Days Ahead for Predatory Animals in Estes Park," *Estes Park Trail* (Estes Park, Colorado: January 6, 1922, vol. 1, no. 39), p. 1.

2. James H. Pickering, *America's Switzerland* (Boulder: University Press of Colorado, 2005), p. 300.

3. Ibid., p. 327.

4. Janet Thayer, "Tunnel Vision," *Loveland Reporter Herald,* June 22, 1997.

Chapter 4. Life in the Park

1. John C. Emerick, *Rocky Mountain National Park Natural History Handbook* (Niwot, Colo.: Rocky Mountain Nature Association, 1995), p. 104.

2. U.S. Fish and Wildlife Service, "Greenback Cutthroat Trout," *National Fish Hatchery System,* n.d., <http://www.fws.gov/fisheries/nfhs/cutthroat.htm> (July 3, 2007).

3. National Park Service, "Birds," *Rocky Mountain National Park,* n.d., <http://www.nps.gov/romo/naturescience/birds.htm> (July 3, 2007).

4. Ibid.

Chapter 5. Challenges to the Park

1. "The National Park System Caring for the American Legacy," *The National Park Service,* n.d., <http://www.nps.gov/legacy/mission.html> (July 3, 2007).

2. "Rocky Mountain National Park Fact Sheet," *Virtual Courthouse: Larimer County Colorado,* March 28, 2007, <http://www.larimer.org/bcc/April1707/RMNPUpdateweb.htm> (July 3, 2007).

3. Michelle Nijhuis, "Global Warming's Unlikely Harbingers," *HighCountryNews.org,* July 19, 2004, pp. 1–10, <http://www.usu.edu/beetle/documents/HCNarticle.pdf> (July 3, 2007).

4. "Crown Jewels at Risk: Global Warming Threatens Western National Parks," *National Resources Defense Council,* n.d., <http://www.nrdc.org/land/parks/globalwarming/rockymountain.asp> (July 3, 2007).

5. Ibid.

6. Ibid.

7. Rich Bray, "Butterflies," *Rocky Mountain National Park,* August 29, 2006, <http://www.nps.gov/romo/naturescience/butterflies.htm> (June 14, 2007).

8. Todd Hartman, "Park Nitrogen levels twice 'critical load,'" *Rocky Mountain News,* June 1, 2006, p. 1.

9. Ibid.

10. Michael Jamison, "Nonprofits Ponder Role in National Parks Funding," *Missoulian.com,* n.d., <http://www.missoulian.com/articles/2004/12/28/news/mtregional/news03.txt> (July 3, 2007).

11. "Budget Policies Harm Our National Parks," *Scripps Howard News Service,* May 3, 2006, <http://www.shns.com/shns/g_index2cfm?action=detail&pk=EDPARKS-05-03-06> (July 3, 2007).

12. "Park Services Slashed, Memos Instruct Staff to Mislead Media," *Environment News Service,* March 18, 2004, <http://www.ens-newswire.com/ens/mar2004/2004-03-18-01.asp> (July 3, 2007).

13. "Fact Sheet: The National Parks Centennial Initiative," *The White House,* n.d., <http://www.whitehouse.gov/news/releases/2007/02/20070207.html> (July 3, 2007).

Chapter 6. What First?

1. "Ten Most Visited National Parks, 2006" *InfoPlease,* 2007, http://www.infoplease.com/science/environment/most-visited-parks-2006.html (July 15, 2008).

2. Dougald MacDonald, *Longs Peak: The Story of Colorado's Favorite Fourteener* (Englewood, Colo.: Westcliffe Publishers, 2004), p. 136.

Bograd, Larry. *The Rocky Mountains.* New York: Benchmark Books, 2001.

Feinstein, Stephen. *The Bighorn Sheep: Help Save This Endangered Species!* Berkeley Heights, N.J.: MyReportLinks.com Books, 2008.

Grupper, Johnathan. *Destination: Rocky Mountain.* Washington, D.C.: National Geographic Society, 2001.

Hall, M.C. *Rocky Mountain National Park.* Chicago: Heinemann Library, 2006.

Harris, Tim. *Mountains and Highlands.* Austin, Tex.: Raintree Steck-Vaughn, 2003.

Lynch, Wayne and Aubrey Lang. *Rocky Mountains.* Minnetonka, Minn.: North Word Books, 2006.

Maynard, Charles W. *The Rocky Mountains.* New York: PowerKids Press, 2004.

Parker, Ron. *Rocky Mountain Wildlife.* Vancouver, B.C.: Raincoast, 200.

Pfaffmanm, Garrick. *Rocky Mountain Mammals.* Basalt, Colo.: Bearbop Press, 2006.

Wrobel, Scott. *Elk.* North Mankato, Minn.: Smart Apple Media, 2001.

WITHDRAWN